MARCUS BINNEY · ROSY RUNCIMAN

GLYNDEBOURNE

Building a Vision

INTRODUCTION BY SIR GEORGE CHRISTIE

With 175 illustrations, 61 in colour

THAMES AND HUDSON

Opposite. *A summer evening on the ha-ha lawn at Glyndebourne by Sir Hugh Casson PPRA*

CONTENTS

Introduction

BUILDING A THEATRE devoted to the performance of opera has been, generally speaking, a rare occurrence in the past 100 years – that is, of course, outside Germany. As a result, there is not a great deal to go on in terms of recent architectural pedigree. You have to look back to the 19th century when a considerable number of opera houses sprang up, the best of which originated in style and design from the finest models of the 18th century, such as the Fenice in Venice and the Markgräfliches in Bayreuth. These models threw up in Europe some of the most beautiful buildings to be constructed since architectural endeavours focussed on the construction of cathedrals, abbeys, etc.

When my father set out to construct his opera house, he looked to Wagner's Festspielhaus in Bayreuth as his model. Mind you, he copied remarkably little of that marvellous opera house. He built a 'shoe box' auditorium rather than the fan-shape which Wagner went for. And he opted for an auditorium which, as it turned out, had a particular characteristic of the 17th century Venetian opera houses, namely having the apex of the cyclorama as far from the orchestra pit (60 feet) as the back wall of the auditorium – a huge asset for directors who frequently enjoyed and exploited this considerable stage depth and which remained unchanged from almost the start of the old theatre's life until its end. However, he adapted and changed constantly and passionately all the other dimensions of his theatre. The auditorium was repeatedly expanded – from some 300 seats to some 800, all within the original roof structure – and pretty dotty it became in terms of sight-lines (given the immoveable width of the proscenium arch) and acoustics. We lived with this state of affairs for most of my 57 years of life and most people loved the home-spun building to which they had become accustomed. I too had a deep affection for it; but for some time had become increasingly aware that, if Glyndebourne was to survive with any hope of a long-term future, it had to 'grasp the nettle by the throat' (as my sister used to say) and have a proper opera house.

On the positive side, the objectives for building the new theatre were principally to generate more revenue as a result of the increased seating

George and Mary Christie on site during the early stages of construction work, February 1992

7

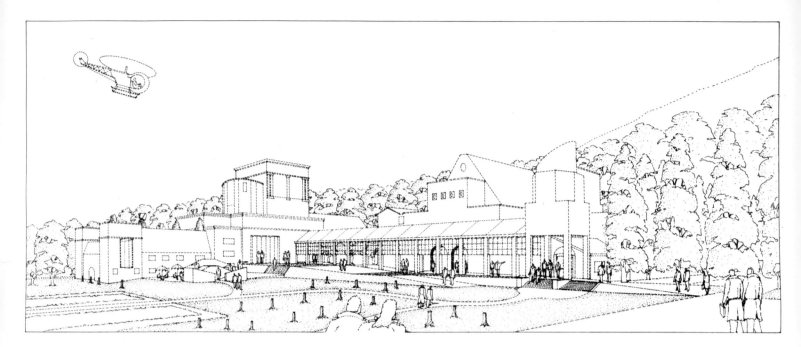

Design by James Stirling, Michael Wilford and Laurence Bain for the new Glyndebourne, retaining the old Opera House as a restaurant and bar, 1989

capacity and so help to ensure Glyndebourne's future in the longer term. It was always an imperative in the development of the plans that the building should (despite the 50% increase in seating capacity) provide a strong sense of intimacy, should have vastly improved acoustics, should not be plush but rather contextual (whilst making its own architectural statement), should meet modern technical requirements without going overboard in the process; and – if this collective imperative was met – the new opera house should provide fulfilment to performers, technicians and other members of the company as well as to audiences at a level far higher than could be expected in the old house.

On the negative side, the old building was in truth on its last legs. It was functionally unable to meet artistic and technical competition. It was architecturally a hotch-potch. And it failed in terms of auditorium size to meet audience demand.

English Heritage visited the old building in autumn 1989 and pronounced that, were we to go ahead with the rebuild, they would not stand in the way and that there was nothing worth preserving architecturally.

There was a good deal of opposition to the news that the old building might be replaced with a new one. It was for this reason that

we allowed a long lead-time of two-and-a-half years to acclimatise people to the idea and in particular to persuade our audiences to take stock of the reasons for needing a replacement. At the end of this period in January 1990 we launched our Appeal and encountered immediately an enthusiastic and generous response – admittedly at a time of a boom economy.

By then we had advanced our architectural plans. We had interviewed nine British architects. (We confined the selection to Britain, firstly because there are many good architects in this country and secondly because it seemed to me that we could land ourselves with a lot of problems if we wanted a close working relationship with someone who, for example, lived in Nicaragua.) From the nine, we selected two architects, Michael Hopkins and James Stirling, and paid each enough money to take us seriously and to provide drawings and a model of their design concepts. These two payments represented the only financial commitment we sought from Glyndebourne Productions Limited in these early stages – and even this commitment stood to be halved as a result of the payment to the winning architect being deductible from his commission, assuming of course the building went ahead. Hopkins, as is now well-known, won this limited competition.

We also at this stage made a wise decision – to construct the new

Drawing of the opera house from across the lawn by Michael Hopkins and Partners, 1993

9

theatre in two stages, the first falling outside the confines of the old building and the second of course being located on the foot-print of the old building. This threw up a number of advantages, by far the largest of which was limitation of the loss of Festival seasons. We were able, during the period October 1991 to August 1992, to advance the building works by constructing something like one quarter of the new theatre – and accordingly lost only the 1993 Festival.

I suppose the three chief anxieties I had when we embarked on the rebuild were:

i.   Would we raise the money – £33 million?
ii. Would we be able to complete the building without an over-run which would, in the event that we were to lose the whole or part of a second Festival, have had disastrous consequences?
iii. Would we have a beautiful building?

At the time of writing it looks, in answer to these questions, as if we are getting close to our funding target; we are going to complete on schedule, thanks to the rigorously controlled construction management by Bovis and by our Project Manager, Eric Gabriel; and we are going to have an opera house of significant architectural importance.

What is more, now that the theatre is detached from my house (the old theatre was attached), my family and I can no longer be categorised as living in a 'semi'.

SIR GEORGE CHRISTIE
October 1993

The flytower about to be lifted off the top of the old theatre during demolition, August 1992

1

*Manor
to
Mansion*

'Perhaps he'll say, viewing my cell beneath,
(Where I began, and where will cease to breath,)
Here liv'd the man, who to these fair retreats
First drew the Muses from their ancient seats:
Tho' low his thoughts, tho' impotent his strain,
Yet let me never of his song complain:
For this the fruitless labour recommends,
He lov'd his native country and his friends.'

From Mount Caburn by *William Hay*[1]

SURPRISE is most people's reaction on seeing Glyndebourne for the first time. Its international reputation leads one to expect a grand, imposing residence rather than an unassuming country mansion. The lack of pretension about the twentieth-century house is symbolic of the whole of John Christie's approach in founding Glyndebourne Festival Opera. The emphasis throughout the theatre and in his own home was on comfort without fuss.

John Christie was a man of vision, talented, wealthy, kind, eccentric and a practical joker. He derived great pleasure from telling exaggerated stories about his life and the events in it. The history of Glyndebourne was not exempt from these flights of fancy and he delighted in taking people to a spot behind the oldest part of the house and regaling them with lively tales about its early history as an Anglo-Saxon burial ground.[2] He had no doubt read of the hill overlooking Glyndebourne where six or seven Anglo-Saxon skeletons were found:

> They had been carefully interred at a depth of 4 or 5 feet, and each had a knife in the left hand, while most of them were surrounded by a circle of large flints, placed with great care around the body.[3]

In characteristic fashion, John Christie 'improved' the story by moving the site to Glyndebourne itself.

In the same way he would have derived wry amusement from another fable about the house, unwittingly perpetuated from 1868 until after his death in 1962. History relates that Glyndebourne was part of the adjoining Glynde Place Estate, which came into the Hay family when John Hay married Mary Morley of Glynde Place in 1589 and since that

*The Christie family home seen
from the blue border in 1983*

William Hay (1695–1755), the most famous member of five generations of his family who lived at Glyndebourne from 1618 to 1803

date the property has never been sold.[4] Truth tells a less romantic tale. There is no documentary evidence to indicate that John Hay ever lived at Glyndebourne. His estate was at Herstmonceux and it is in that cemetery that both he and his wife are buried rather than at Glynde where they would surely have been interred if they had been resident at Glyndebourne.

Originally Glyndebourne was part of the nearby Broyle Place Estate, which diminished in size when its owners, the staunchly Catholic Thatcher family, were persecuted in the time of Elizabeth I. In 1606 they sold Glyndebourne to a local yeoman called Nicholas Aptot for £1,200. Aptot kept the property for only three and a half years before selling it at a loss to John Puckle, who lived there until 1618. It was then sold again to John Hay's son, Herbert, as a home for himself and his new wife Frances Culpeper.[5] After having three different owners in the space of twelve years, Glyndebourne now experienced a period of continuity and the Hays prospered and flourished there until 1803, when the family line died out.

From 1610 the name Glyndebourne, literally meaning a glind or valley bordered by a bourne or river, increasingly came into usage. Until then, the house had been known as Wood's Tenement in the Hole after the A'Wood family who lived there when it was part of the Broyle Place Estate. Fortunately for us, a more lyrical name was adopted. Would Wood's Tenement in the Hole Festival Opera ever have attracted such a devoted following?

The exact age of the house is uncertain; inside, some chalk walls, chalk-lined chimneys and a small amount of pre-Tudor panelling point to the early sixteenth century. The fact that Herbert and Frances Hay's first child, Anne, was born on 14 April 1620 at the Culpeper family home in Folkington leads to the supposition that the first in a succession of major alterations was being undertaken at Glyndebourne. Certainly at about this time a large extension was added to the back of the house, which doubled its overall size. The transformation from country house to country mansion had begun.

Herbert Hay's son, John, enhanced the family's standing by becoming the first of four generations of Hays to be Member of Parliament for a local constituency. His status as a representative of the people may have

been a strong influence on his desire to reside in a more fashionable house. At all events, in the mid-seventeeth century Glyndebourne was again increased in size and an imposing façade added to the west front. We have no visual record of the house after these alterations because it was not until about 1756 that a picture was painted by Melchair, revealing a dignified double-bayed house with what appears to be a large conservatory shielding the Elizabethan portion from view. The windmill in the background of this picture, built in 1700, was in regular use until 1921; but it fell into a state of such disrepair that in May 1925 it collapsed.[6]

Glyndebourne painted by Melchair c.1756, showing the house in a setting that is remarkably unchanged today

15

*Glyndebourne, 1868. The white stucco façade was
added by Henrietta and Frances Hay*

*A photograph of the house taken in the early 1870s.
The extension on the right marks the first phase of the
Victorian alterations*

*Right. Watercolour painting of Glyndebourne after the
1870s alterations by Ewan Christian*

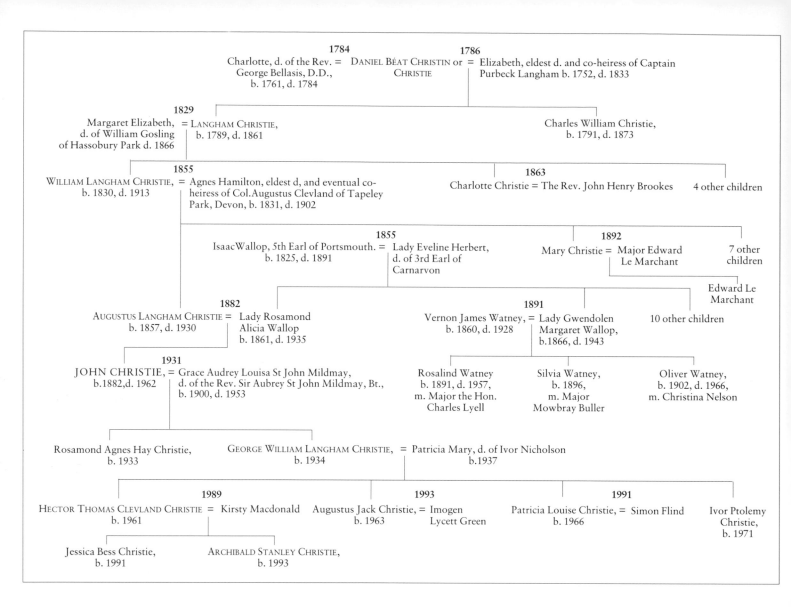

The Christie family tree

John Hay's grandson, William, might be described as the first real character in the Glyndebourne mould. Though born deformed and dwarf-like, he became Member of Parliament for Seaford, Keeper of Records in the Tower of London, Commissioner of the Victualling Office and a diligent manager of his estate. In the preface to William Hay's writings, his daughters, Henrietta and Frances, tell us:

> From the time he began to reside in the country, he turned his thoughts to the improvement of that small part of his estates, which had descended to him from his ancestors. He was kind to his tenants, encouraged agriculture, cultivated gardening in almost all its branches, and was perhaps the first who began to ornament cornfields with walks and plantations.[7]

One of the walks he laid out was a beech walk, which took advantage of the steep incline behind the house to give fine views out over the Downs. Account books from the early 1720s reveal that there were often up to nine labourers working in the garden. Walls and terraces were added and in 1724 much levelling work was done.[8] There is an unsubstantiated story that William Hay bred silkworms in the grounds at Glyndebourne.[9] He was outraged at the high prices that had to be paid to import silk into England and determined to prove that the British could manufacture it themselves. The oldest tree in the garden, a mulberry, would support this were it not for the fact that it is a black mulberry, the leaves of which are unsuitable for silkworms.

None of William Hay's five children married. His daughters Henrietta and Frances managed the estate from 1786 to 1803 and made what were to be the last alterations to the house for almost a century. They extended the southern façade looking over the ha-ha lawn, and introduced what John Christie described as 'Queen Anne' windows and an ornate entrance portico which reflected the vogue for the classical style.

After the death of the Hay sisters, their cousin, the Reverend Francis Tutté, a prebend of Peterborough Cathedral, inherited Glyndebourne. He lived there for twenty years and was noted in the locality for his kind and cheerful disposition. In 1824 he died at the age of 94. Disputes now arose as to who was the rightful heir to Glyndebourne. Henrietta and Frances Hay and the Reverend Tutté had left differing wills, one stipulating that the Langhams (one of Herbert Hay's daughters, Sarah, had married Sir John Langham in 1650) should inherit the estate and another less specifically stating that it should pass to the descendants of Herbert Hay.

In about 1824 James Hay Langham settled at Glyndebourne. He enjoyed the country life and took great pleasure in the pack of harriers he kept on the estate to control the local hare population. However, one condition of his succeeding to his father's baronetcy and Northamptonshire estates in 1833 was that he should relinquish Glyndebourne. Lengthy litigation followed between the two principal claimants, Langham Christie, a second cousin of James Hay Langham, and Mr Sanford of Nynehead Court in Somerset who was a direct descendant of Herbert Hay. The case was won by Langham Christie, who became the first of five generations of Christies to live at Glyndebourne.

Ewan Christian (1814–95), architect of the Victorian additions at Glyndebourne

19

The Christie family coat of arms in the Organ Room at Glyndebourne. The motto 'Integer vitae' is from an ode by Horace meaning 'He that is unstained in life and pure from guilt'

Langham Christie made some small additions to the house – the most notable being a fives court, later to become the site of the Organ Room – but it was his son William Langham Christie who made more dramatic alterations. Using money from the sale of the family home, Preston Deanery in Northamptonshire, he changed the appearance of Glyndebourne and vastly increased the size of the estate from 1,500 to 10,500 acres.

The alterations took place in two phases. In about 1870 the conservatory was replaced by a substantial brick-built extension, which hid much of the early seventeenth-century façade from view. Then, in 1876, an architect named Ewan Christian was engaged to make improvements. He was known mostly for his ecclesiastical architecture, and also for his designs for the National Portrait Gallery. Like Sir John Soane he placed great emphasis on the introduction of light into a room, though with considerably less imaginative flair than that of his predecessor.

> He delighted in providing what he called a 'sun-trap', some projecting bay or window in a canted angle to admit a few rays into a room which without it would, from its aspect, have been deprived of them.[10]

At Glyndebourne he added a bay window to a room on the south façade, which in recent times has been used as an office by conductors. His other alterations included cladding the exterior with quantities of decorated brickwork, reflecting the fashion for Tudor-Old English. The concurrent interest in the Gothic had already been an influence in the turret added to the front of the house in 1870 and the ornate stonework and balustrades added to the south and west façades. William Christie's sister thought the result 'restless and the brick aggressive'.[11] Modern-day opinion is divided, on the one hand describing the effect as 'sophisticated and lively',[12] and on the other as having 'little that Mozart could have liked about it'.[13] John Christie thought the 'Victorianisation' hideous and the height of bad taste. Certainly one or two photographs taken towards the end of the last century do suggest it would have been an ideal set for a Gothic horror film. The air of desolation and neglect clearly indicates why Christie was so keen to begin modernization.

'I don't yet know *what* I am going to do, but I shall
find out. I want to make the world a better and a happier place.'
John Christie to W.E. Edwards, May 1920 [1]

JOHN CHRISTIE was born in December 1882 at Eggesford, North Devon,
the home of his maternal grandfather. He was the only child of a love-
less and unhappy marriage between Augustus Langham Christie and
Lady Rosamond Alicia Wallop. Beginning in October 1882, Augustus
Christie suffered from periods of derangement. It seems likely that the
first of these fits was brought on at the sight of his wife's pregnant figure,
and for her own safety Lady Rosamond was obliged to spend much time
away from her husband. As a result John Christie had a difficult child-
hood, finding more happiness and stability with his mother's sister Lady
Margaret Watney and her husband than with either of his parents. Out
of these adverse circumstances, he appears to have gained the strength
that was to lead to his success.

After the death in 1913 of his grandfather, William Langham Christie,
John Christie spent a good deal of time in Sussex. His father preferred to
live at Tapeley, the family estate in Devon, and was happy to grant his son
the use of Glyndebourne. From that date until 1922, when Christie gave
up his job as a science master at Eton to manage the estate full-time,
Glyndebourne was his vacation and weekend home and an increasing
passion in his life.

It was after he was invalided out of the army in 1916 that Christie
began to make changes to the house. At first the changes were cosmetic:
rooms were redecorated and furniture, carpets, curtains and paintings
removed and replaced. He had as little time for reproduction furniture
and paintings inside as he had for the mock-Tudor and Gothic exterior.
He told his mother: 'The house is too big for reproductions and the only
thing is the genuine article.'[2]

Gradually more major alterations began. New bathrooms were fitted
with a 'superb'[3] hot water supply; electric light was installed for which
just over two hundred lamps were required; a nineteenth-century 'jerry

John Christie, c.1920

Above left. *Three generations of the Christie family at Glyndebourne, 1895. From left: John Christie (1882–1962); his grandfather, William Langham (1830–1913); and his father, Augustus Langham (1857–1930)*

Above right. *The drawing room at Glyndebourne, 1893*

built'[4] wing containing a small servants hall, dark pantry and the sitting room of Childs the butler was demolished and replaced by a two-storey building with kitchen area beneath and housekeeper's flat above; garages and hot houses were constructed; the brick-and-stone archway under which everyone passes on arrival at Glyndebourne was erected 'to help the frontage to the road'.[5] By 1923 the interior was more or less the way John Christie wanted it, and he needed a new scheme to occupy his mind – the exterior.

This period of Glyndebourne's history is well documented in the frequent letters Christie wrote to his mother, who constantly upbraided him for his expenditure. Of his plans for the exterior, he wrote to her, 'I don't want to make it into a palace but architecturally the porch and the spike [Gothic style turret] are frightfully ugly and this is primarily my object in the alteration.'[6] Like all his schemes, it began simply and, as he took pains to reassure Lady Rosamond, would cost little, but it quickly became more grandiose. The removal of the porch and turret grew into the addition of two small rooms, the transformation of the hall and drawing room into a large front hall, the extension of the dining room, the building of a new entrance hall with a cellar beneath and the removal of all the decorated brickwork from the south and west façades. In fact, by 1925 the house had become the one we know today.

John Christie's purpose in all these changes was not just to make life more agreeable for himself and his house guests, of whom there were a constant stream; he also possessed a strong sense of altruism and duty towards the local community. In December 1918 he wrote:

> The room next to my study is very comfortable & I am thinking of using it as a reading room for Ringmer & Glynde . . . Books, a fire, comfortable chairs and tea. I have also a plan for starting lectures on various subjects such as are being given to the troops, their object being in my opinion to stimulate interest in intellectual matters.[7]

Later he commented, with some surprise, on how much the room was being used by the public.

His sense of duty towards the local community extended much further than this. As Glyndebourne absorbed more of his time, he gradually purchased and developed nearby companies to help run the estate. He took great pleasure in his creation of a twentieth-century feudal system by which he provided employment for a large number of people who in return worked loyally for him for the majority of their lives.

The range of his activities was daunting. While still an Eton science master, he was overseeing all the changes to the house, taking an active interest in his farms, livestock, timber business and forge, acting as a director of both Ringmer Motor Works, which he purchased in 1919, and

Above left. A sketch by John Christie proposing the archway, now familiar to many as the entrance to the Opera House

Above right. The house after John Christie's alterations in the 1920s and as it still looks today

23

Watercolour by Sir Hugh Casson of the Organ Room, which he described as 'a magnificent Rookery-Nookish hall'

Opposite. *The Organ Room, showing the gallery where members of the audience sat for concerts and recitals. The panelling in the gallery is* trompe l'oeil, *painted by John Christie in 1943*

Ringmer Building Works, which began life servicing the estate and grew into a major south-eastern company, and advising his parents about the running of the family estate at Tapeley. Only occasionally did he long for peace and complain that there were at least twenty workmen climbing all over different parts of his house; in general he thrived on the variety.

Of all his projects, the one that excited him most and was to bring him greatest pleasure was the building of the Organ Room. As early as 1917 he was considering building this room. He had a great friend, Dr Charles Harford Lloyd, then nearing retirement, who had been precentor at Eton and subsequently became Organist at the Chapel Royal in St James's. The story goes that Christie wanted him to retire to Ringmer, but Lloyd

Employees of John Christie's company, Ringmer Building Works, roofing the Organ Room in 1920

Right. *James Robertson, the Chorus Master, rehearsing the chorus in the Organ Room, with George Austin at the piano, 16 May 1939*

refused to do so unless there was a first-class organ there for him to play. In characteristic fashion, Christie set about remedying this situation.

He selected Edmond Warre as his architect, Ringmer Building Works as constructors, Dr Lloyd as his adviser on organs and Hill, Norman and Beard as his organ builders. At first he was undecided about whether to modify the fives court at the south-west end of the house or turn it into a long gallery, placing the organ at one end. A further alternative was to put the organ into a pantry, having first lowered the floor by eight feet. Gradually his ideas crystallized: the five courts would have to be demolished, because '(a) it is useless (b) ugly'[8], and the Organ Room built in its place. His mother was horrified at the thought of what his latest scheme would cost. He tried to mollify her by telling her how much good it would do for musical education and how he would be able to give recitals to raise money for charitable purposes. However, by the time the Organ Room was completed it had cost in the region of £18,000 to build, panel and furnish, and install the organ and its case – a figure which today would be the equivalent of almost £300,000. It must be considered as worth every penny, for without the Organ Room it is unlikely that Glyndebourne Festival Opera would have come about as we know it.

The architect Edmond Warre had been a friend of John Christie's for many years, as had his brother Felix. They were sons of Dr Edmond Warre, a famous Headmaster and Provost at Eton, and affectionately known as White Bear and Brown Bear.[10] In Edmond's case the nickname stuck and John Christie always called him 'Bear' Warre. He had his own architectural practice and had carried out alterations to other country houses, such as Wilton House, where he degothicized the library.[11] He and John Christie together had worked on the first phase of the alterations to Glyndebourne and by March 1919 the plans for the Organ Room were sufficiently far advanced for Christie to tell his mother,

> It will be a long, narrow and high room, perhaps with a long bow window on the lawn side and two high windows on either side of it. It will be panelled with oak to a height of about 11 feet and the organ will be at the far end. There will be a gallery at the house end where the servants can listen and anyone from Ringmer or Glynde.[12]

The room they created was eighty feet long and thus almost double the length of the southern façade of the house. Christie was always very

Dr Charles Harford Lloyd, with whom John Christie travelled extensively in the early 1900s to attend operas, particularly at Munich and Bayreuth

John Christie in costume for his role as Beckmesser. Steuart Wilson – Von Stolzing in the programme for 3 June 1928 – later became Music Director of the Arts Council and Director of BBC Music

conscious of trying to create buildings in keeping with their surroundings. The Organ Room was built in traditional Bath stone and red brick, which toned well with the subsequent simplifications of the rest of the exterior, and the large bay window and balustrade along the parapet mirrored those added by Ewan Christian in 1876.

One individual feature of the Organ Room after the opera house was built was the entrance to it. Visitors approached from the red foyer through a standard oak-panelled door and bowed their heads to walk under a stone arch (the elaborate frontage to a recessed fireplace), then, as they stretched upright, they uttered a gasp of surprise and amazement. There is nothing else at Glyndebourne to prepare you for the grandeur and beauty of this room. The oak panelling, plaster-work ceiling with its hanging pendants, mullioned windows inset with ancestral coats of arms and suffused light create a feeling of the 1580s rather than the 1920s, and the atmosphere is one of complete tranquillity.

The organ itself is similar in scale to a cathedral organ and occupies the full width of the room and a quarter of its length. Initially Hill, Norman and Beard followed Dr Lloyd's specifications, but when he died just as the organ was almost completed, their problems began. While John Christie had learned a great deal about organ building, going so far as to purchase a controlling interest in Hill, Norman and Beard when Dr A.G. Hill died, he was by no means an expert. He tended to invite specialists down for weekends, pick their brains about his organ and then request modifications according to the advice they had given him. The result was that the instrument was never entirely satisfactory.

The Organ Room became the venue for many concerts and operatic performances, which were attended largely by local people. John Christie took an active role in these events. He played the part of Antonio, the gardener, in *Le nozze di Figaro*, Beckmesser in *Die Meistersinger* and on occasion clashed the cymbals at recitals. More importantly, it was when a young singer called Audrey Mildmay came to Glyndebourne in December 1930 to sing the part of Blonde in *Die Entführung* that Christie met his future wife. He fell in love with her instantly. At the end of her visit he took her upstairs to one of the bedrooms and announced, 'This is where we will sleep when we are married.' Understandably, she was less certain. It was an unlikely match; John Christie was a hitherto confirmed

bachelor of 47 and she a beautiful singer, seventeen years his junior, enjoying a successful career. In courtship as in all other aspects of his life, Christie was determined to succeed. He pursued her avidly, showered her with generous gifts, and within six months he had won her over. They were married on 4 June 1931 at Queen Camel in Somerset and a new era in Glyndebourne's history began.

The ambience of the Organ Room reflected in John Gunter's set for Lady Billows' house in Britten's opera Albert Herring, *1985*

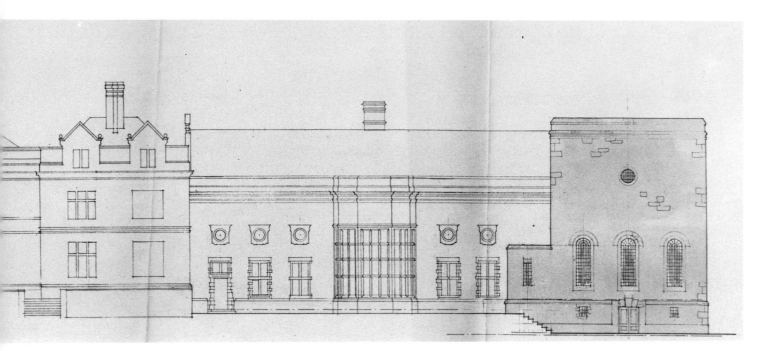

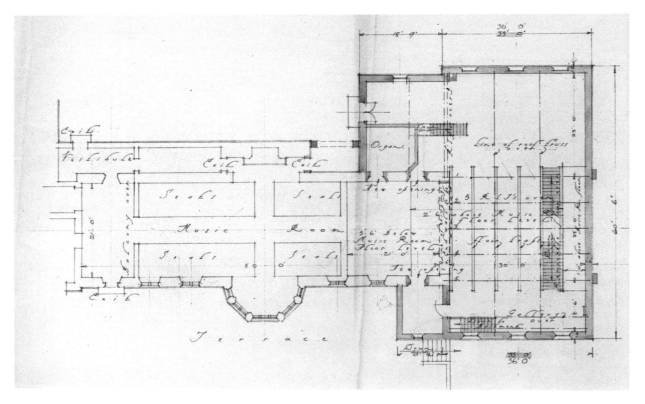

The original, unexecuted, plans for the theatre at Glyndebourne, in which the main body of the Organ Room became the auditorium and the organ itself was moved to make way for the stage and backstage areas

3

THROUGHOUT the 1920s John Christie had become increasingly interested in the theatre in general and opera in particular. At home, his plans for recitals and concerts in the Organ Room became more ambitious; then in 1925 he took the lease on the Opera House in Tunbridge Wells, and really began to find out about running a theatre. When he attended opera in Germany or Austria, he absorbed all the details, realized that the artistic and technical standards abroad far exceeded those in Britain, and when the time came to build his own opera house was determined to surpass them.

Christie's growing interest in the theatre and in music took flight upon his marriage to Audrey Mildmay in June 1931. By September of that year he had already commissioned an architect, J.W. Wilcox, to draw up plans to build a stage and two months later work was in progress. The first set of drawings was for an addition to the Organ Room: the end wall of this room was to be removed and a stage built stretching back 30 feet, with a small backstage area behind. The organ would have been dismantled and rebuilt to one side of the new orchestra pit and the seating within the room rearranged in four blocks at stalls level with the gallery above. This design would have enabled the Organ Room recitals, concerts, operatic extracts and theatricals to continue on a grander scale – a small traditional country house theatre for the amusement of weekend guests and the entertainment of the local community. Fortunately, Audrey Mildmay realized that it was not enough and said to her husband in words now famous in musical history, 'If you're going to spend all that money, John, for God's sake do the thing properly!' The plans were quickly changed and the stage, although still situated at the far end of the Organ Room, was turned through 90° to face north with a new, much larger, auditorium beyond. Apart from enthusiasm, one of the reasons for rushing headlong into this ambitious scheme was finance. England had abandoned the Gold Standard on 21 September 1931 and there was a deep-seated fear that rapid devaluation was to follow. The theatre had to be built while it was still an affordable proposition. By the beginning of November 1931 work was well under way – typically of Christie, before he had been granted official approval.

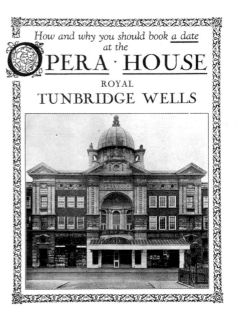

Promotional leaflet for the 1926 season. The performances were to include Alice in Wonderland, Cuckoo in the Nest, *presented by the D'Oyly Carte, and* Katja the Dancer

The stage construction is started. It is being built at the end of the Organ Room with a barn up the hill for auditorium. We are using all our bricks and stone from the yard and having a general clearance. We are buying old bricks where we can and overburnt and crooked stock bricks. The walls are to be built rough and the stage walls are not to be plastered. It will have a flat roof of boards covered with a tarred and sanded felt which we used in the Lewes school.[2]

One wonders how such a building, constructed of essentially second-class and second-hand materials, remained standing for sixty years. The answer is that during that period so many changes were made that little of the original structure was actually still *in situ* by 1992.

The theatre was rectangular in shape with an elegant classical façade facing the lawns. The angularity of this façade balanced the sharply pointed gables on the house itself and, by 1934, the already mellowed second-hand brick and sandstone gave the appearance of an older building. Inside, the 300-seat auditorium was on one level, with a raised box at the back containing a further eleven seats. That hallmark of a Christie room, oak panelling, surrounded the patrons on three sides with an uncarpeted floor beneath their feet. The three-armed lighting brackets had been designed by Christie himself in collaboration with W.J. (Bill) Thorpe, Managing Director of his motor company, Ringmer Motor Works. As always, he recounted the expenditure on these brackets to his mother –

View to the south of the Organ Room, showing the kitchen garden where the theatre was built

cost about £1 each without lamps and 4 ½d (about 2p) per hour to run. The comfortable brown seats were raked and carefully positioned to alternate, ensuring that nobody was sitting directly behind someone else. Christie's philanthropic streak was evident in the provision of four free seats for the blind tucked away in one of the lighting boxes. Fortunately someone, perhaps Audrey, had prevailed upon Christie to have a proper roof with a barrel vaulted ceiling rather than boards covered with felt, which would have allowed all extraneous sounds to penetrate the auditorium. It was a simple country theatre in keeping with its surroundings. Gilded jewel boxes were for the city.

Inevitably the speed of the work meant that short cuts were taken and mistakes made. There were no proper foundations and right to the end of the theatre's life it was said that you could lift floorboards in the auditorium and see chalk immediately beneath. Space for scenery storage was an aspect almost completely overlooked. Throughout the first season the only way to change the sets was to take one out through the wings into the garden and bring the next in from the lawns. There were insufficient facilities for the singers; one dressing room for the principal men and one for the principal women may have been acceptable for an amateur production and may have created a spirit of bonhomie, but it was not something to which singers of the calibre of Willi Domgraf-Fassbänder (Figaro) and Luise Helletsgruber (Cherubino) were accustomed. The orchestra pit seated only half the sixty musicians that Christie claimed, thus limiting, in retrospect beneficially, the range of operas that could be produced and excluding the composer closest to John Christie's heart – Wagner.

These defects indicate the hand of an amateur who, although he sought help and advice from Edmond Warre, took pride in the fact that he was essentially his own architect.

> I am pleased with the general appearance and the general lay out. It may be advertised with me as architect! It would be funny if as a result I were asked to architect something else![3]

Considering his complete lack of architectural training, the defects were remarkably few. By May 1932, only six months after serious work had begun, the decorations in the auditorium were complete with the exception of the oak panelling and the flooring. The fundamental building

The classical façade of the Opera House designed by Edmond Warre, 1934

Above and opposite. *Two photographs of the theatre interior looking towards the stage and towards the Christie family box. The picture above shows the proscenium arch and surround before it was painted black. The set on stage is an experimental one designed by Hamish Wilson*

work done, a long period now followed during which Christie indulged his passion for stage mechanisms.

His training as a science master led to a fascination with all technical aspects of the theatre, especially lighting and stage effects. His ideas for lighting came from visits to opera houses on the Continent where he nearly always asked to go backstage to 'see the stage arrangements', a phrase which meant having as many as possible of the techniques relating to lights, special effects and movement of scenery operated for his benefit. The technical facilities which resulted at Glyndebourne were a combination of his own scientific skills in adapting the equipment he had seen demonstrated and the practical abilities of his work force in converting his instructions into reality.

Christie wanted to have the lighting boxes situated in a place where the technicians could see the stage and respond to events happening on it.

This led to one box being placed in a raised position at each side of the front of the auditorium. The stage lighting system chosen was invented by an Italian, Bordoni, who sold the idea to Germany where it had just begun to be used to great effect in Danzig. John Christie and Bill Thorpe designed their own lighting switchboard, which had dimming possibilities never seen before in Britain. In all respects, Christie was aided by the practical experience of his wife, who wrote to him from Vienna where she was taking singing lessons:

> By the way what are you doing for spot-lighting a single figure – I mean for instance Loge who has a firey light the whole evening which follows him wherever he goes.[4]

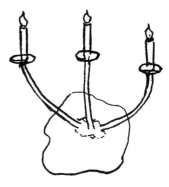

Sketch for one of the lighting brackets by John Christie

He took note of her comments, assured her nothing would be overlooked and then went on to describe his pulley mechanism for raising and lowering the lighting bars, the cost of the cyclorama cloth and some armour he had purchased which might be useful for *Parsifal*.[5]

Hope Bagenal, acoustic adviser to John Christie, who described Christie as coming into the 'category of mysterium tremendum *rather than that of an ordinary client'*

Stage gadgetry, such as wind machines, steam boilers to create stage fires and cloud apparati, were all specially adapted for Glyndebourne. Where others might have grown faint-hearted, John Christie was never happier than when he was working alongside his employees tackling the latest problem that had arisen.

These problems could not have been overcome without strong support from Christie's other businesses. He enjoyed the challenge of obtaining a quote, for example, for theatre seating or the lighting switchboard, deciding it was outrageously expensive and then using his own work force to create something better for less money. 'It is more fun & we shall get what we want.'[6] He was fortunate to have dedicated managers like Bill Thorpe and Bernard Sharp, Managing Director of his local construction company, Ringmer Building Works, together with a host of loyal employees and his trusted advisers, the architect 'Bear' Warre, the acoustician Hope Bagenal, the designer and stage manager Hamish Wilson and Herbert Norman of his organ-building company Hill, Norman & Beard.

Bill Thorpe was an extremely capable electrician who worked all hours, first to understand and then to execute Christie's complicated demands based on lighting systems Thorpe himself had not seen. Some of the items he developed include the lighting circuits, the motor gear needed to raise the proscenium curtain, the lighting switchboard and the pressure-painting plant for scenery.

Bernard Sharp, together with John Christie, arranged details such as the fixing of the cyclorama, which was not at this point a permanent feature. It had to be hung from a specially constructed circular rail and moved into position with a complicated series of ropes and pulleys. Sharp was also responsible for having plans drawn up, e.g., for the scenery store, and later for the additional dining hall, the dressing rooms and the chauffeurs' room.

The employees were expected to become jacks of all trades. Erne Daniels, the housekeeper's husband, would one day be bricklaying, the next concreting the understage area and the next moving soil displaced when the roadway between the house and the opera house was straightened.

Arthur Parsons and his boy, Reg Tribe, were noted for their agility:

Parsons and his boy have been working at dizzying heights on the stage. They walk about carelessly on those girders steadying themselves by touching the roof above them with their hands. They sit down on the counterweight girder holding on by a foot turned round one of the lattices of the girder beneath them. Nothing behind them & only a wall three feet away in front of them. Then reaching out to the wall in front (3ft away) they spring up off their bottoms on to their feet & walk down to the ladder 5yds away along the girder![7]

These people and others from Ringmer Building Works, Ringmer Motor Works, Hill, Norman and Beard, the local, family-owned smithy and Plashett timber businesses must by turns have been maddened by Christie's demands (which at times seemed impossible), daunted by the fact that they had no theatrical experience, inspired by his enthusiasm and interest, encouraged when he took note of their advice, challenged by the variety of work and above all excited by the prospect of what they were creating.

Set design by Hamish Wilson for Le nozze di Figaro, *the opening production of the 1934 season*

Programme for the Opera House acoustic test in 1934

Drawing of the conductor Fritz Busch by Kenneth Green, 1937

The overwhelming feeling that emerges from the correspondence of the time is the sense of risk. Such a festival had never been held in Britain before. Unlike John Christie, who never seems to have doubted for a moment that it would succeed, members of his staff were prepared to put endless time and energy into the creation of this very special enterprise, but they were less certain of the outcome.

By May 1933 John Christie could write to his mother:

> We have started on the scenery. We have a model stage in the housekeeper's room. Our stage manager [Hamish Wilson] is here for a few weeks work on *Don Giovanni* and *Walküre*. We are asking Beecham and his orchestra to undertake 4 performances at our opening next year. The orchestra would I suppose be about 70.[8]

In January 1934 this had been modified to an opening season in May consisting of *Così fan tutte* and *Le nozze di Figaro*, with a second season planned for September when *Don Giovanni* and *Die Entführung* would be conducted by Beecham. These two references, separated by seven months, are the first to any musical considerations. Even after the Christies had met their future Musical Director, Fritz Busch, at the end of January 1934, John Christie was still absorbed with technical and aesthetic details such as roofing the dining hall and building the scenery for *Figaro*.

Fritz Busch, a refugee from the Nazi regime, had agreed to conduct Mozart at Glyndebourne, thinking that such a mad scheme could only last one year. He did insist, however, that for that year a good producer should be employed, an idea unusual in England at that time. When Max Reinhardt refused Christie's offer, another refugee from the Nazis, Carl Ebert, was asked. He and Busch came to Glyndebourne in February 1934 and were captivated by it, but also alarmed by the theatre's defects, such as the inability to fly scenery. Nevertheless, they decided to embark on this 'crazy' venture.[9]

In March there was a trial run of the opera house. Boyd Neel and his orchestra were invited down to play three one-act operas, Mozart's *Bastien and Bastienne*, Pergolesi's *La serva padrona* and Bach's *The Coffee Cantata*. As a result the proscenium wall was repainted; it had been the same cream colour as the ceiling and was found to reflect too much light from the music stands in the orchestra pit.

Our latest success here in the Opera House is outstanding. We have finished the decoration of the Proscenium Wall. Dull black or very dark blue. It looks just like rich velvet but is cheap paper. The effect is wonderfully good. It makes the auditorium look bigger, it shows off the curtains and the stage pictures & it reveals more clearly the curves & proportions of the building itself. Audrey opposed it for a year and is now overwhelmed by its beauty.[10]

The theatre in 1936, with scenery by Hamish Wilson for Act III Scene 2 of Le nozze di Figaro, *the Great Hall of the Palazzo, on stage*

Although there were still many details to be finalized, with the structural work completed and the majority of his stage gadgetry in place John

Christie began to promote his creation. From March 1934 onwards there was increasing press coverage in national and local newspapers. Many critics and journalists were given personal guided tours of the theatre, among them Neville Cardus and Francis Toye. All were treated to detailed explanations of the lighting system and stage effects, which clearly baffled them. As Professor F.H. Shera wrote in the *Sheffield Fete*:

> Electrical technicalities have formed no part of the writer's education. The whole of the narrow chamber seemed more like a telephone exchange than anything – innumerable plugs and sockets, yards of rubber-tubing. But we heard with (I hope) due respect a discourse from which the main points emerging were that the system was introduced in Europe only last year, at Vienna and Danzig, and that, in its present form, it could be worked by two men instead of twenty.[11]

To hold the first Glyndebourne Festival three months after the appointment of Fritz Busch and Carl Ebert is a feat that could not be achieved today when singers, designers, producers and conductors are all booked years in advance. Much of the credit should go to Rudolf Bing, a Jew forced to flee from Germany, whose experience of engaging singers was far greater than that of the pedestrian Alfred Nightingale who was appointed as General Manager.

Charles Salvidge plugging up the lighting board, 1934

Ringmer Building Works making the scenery for Don Giovanni, *1936*

On 1 May 1934, with the opening night of Le nozze di Figaro just four weeks away, John Christie wrote to his mother:

> 'We are very busy indeed. There is still a great deal to do. The kitchen plant is to be ordered tomorrow. The range is already on order & sinks. The heating of the kitchen was tested today. All the cloakroom fittings are still to be made. The fire apparatus in the opera house is not started. The lighting is finished except for details about lamps & fittings. The scenery is finished except for odds & ends but there are many of these. The caterers are not yet settled. I am trying to get the Savoy to do it.

This extract makes it very clear where the priorities were – in the theatre. Support services such as cloakroom and catering facilities were neglected in the determination to make the theatre right. Herein lay the key to Glyndebourne's success.

So what did the audience find on that first night at Glyndebourne? A special train laid on from Victoria to Lewes, from which point motor coaches transported them to the opera house, a beautiful garden set amidst the Sussex Downs in which to walk before the performance and during the interval, a complimentary gold programme book containing idiosyncratic articles written by John Christie, a family link so close that one room of the house, the Organ Room, was used as the theatre foyer, a simple wood-panelled theatre, an intimate stage which gave an already powerful performance even greater immediacy, an acoustic, not perfect, but better than after subsequent alterations to the theatre, lighting the standard and subtlety of which had not been seen before in England, a dining hall, somewhat cramped perhaps, but serving good food and excellent wines (Christie was to become noted for providing the latter) and cloakrooms marked 'Herren' and 'Damen' (those backstage with doors wide enough for female artists to enter wearing a crinoline). Some of the details may have been last-minute, but everything had been supplied.

This attentive, friendly atmosphere, combined with the skills of Fritz Busch, Carl Ebert and the music coach Jani Strasser in presenting performances of a standard unprecedented in Great Britain, made a deep impression. The critics and the small first-night audience spread the word that Glyndebourne was an event not to be missed. By the second week the theatre was sold out. Immediately the season ended, John Christie began to build on his success.

Members of the audience arriving at Victoria Station, June 1939

The first night of the Glyndebourne Festival, 28 May 1934

Opposite. *The audience in the gardens*

Above. *Roy Henderson (Count), Audrey Mildmay (Susanna) and Aulikki Rautawaara (Countess) in Carl Ebert's production of* Le nozze di Figaro

Left. *The dining hall, seating all 300 members of the audience. The end of the dinner interval was indicated by a trumpeter playing the call from* Fidelio

4

Building on success

'Instead of building an opera house just to do ordinary performances we aimed at supreme heights.'[1]

ONCE AGAIN, using Edmond Warre as his architectural adviser, Christie drew up new plans – this time to extend the cramped artists' facilities. Between May 1934 and May 1935 the singers found themselves upgraded from primitive to luxurious surroundings. Twenty-four dressing rooms complete with showers were built around a grassed courtyard reserved solely for the artists' use. More impressive still was the Tudor-style Green Room to which the dressing rooms led; it was a long oak-panelled chamber with an oriel window at one end positioned to give a sweeping view of the house, gardens and Downs beyond. Light entered softly through latticed windows, creating the right atmosphere for a room in which the artists could relax or warm up before a rehearsal or performance. It was furnished with antiques and paintings from the house, and the unusual light fittings, like multi-dimensional stars, were based on a design Christie had seen in Vienna.

Viewed from the exterior, the style continued the angular theme of earlier extensions. The materials used were a 'plum pudding' mixture of brick and sandstone of which Nikolaus Pevsner did not approve:

> It is a curious ensemble, and as such perhaps best suited to the informalities of the summer intervals between the acts of the operas.[2]

In other parts of the building there was also feverish activity; Christie allowed a favourite ilex tree to be felled to make way for the building of a much-needed scene dock, and additional scenery stores were developed from nearby stables and garages. Mildmay Dining Hall with a chauffeurs' room at the back was erected on the site of the present Nether Wallop restaurant. Like the old dining area, it was a simple design with a red brick-and-tile exterior and undecorated interior. As Christie intended, it had the feeling of a converted barn that had been part of the estate for years rather than a new purpose-built hall. Lastly, what is described rather poetically in the 1935 programme as a 'lighted path to car park' was provided for the safety of patrons.

The Green Room showing the oriel window surrounded by solanum jasminoides, *1983*

Such modifications would have cost a great deal of money, and as a result, plans to extend the backstage area in time for the 1936 season had to be held in abeyance and alterations limited to the provision of additional office space. This restraint was more than compensated for over the winter of 1936/37:

> The Opera House has a small auditorium and will have, at the end of this year [1936], one of the largest stages in England. It covers an area of ground nearly twice as long as Buckingham Palace.[3]

John Christie was a master of these high-flown statements. Later the stage was to become the 'largest in the British Empire'.[4] It is certainly true that with the building of the temporary cyclorama, which by 1938 had become a permanent structure, the stage increased considerably in depth from 37 feet (11 metres) to 60 feet (18 metres). Thus despite the narrow dimension of the proscenium arch, which to a member of the audience made the stage look small, the stage area was in fact sizeable and enabled an intimate room or a spacious garden to be portrayed with equal realism.

The area behind the cyclorama stretching back to the dressing rooms was enclosed and for the first time there was space to store scenery for several operas. Until then, the scene shifters had worked in rather grim conditions:

> There was a scene store as we used to call it . . . at the end of the ladies and gents toilets out in the garden. We had to go down a flight of steps off the stage which was something like 6ft above the ground level outside [and] carry the scenery to and from this scenery store in all winds and weather, many a time we were soaking wet through.[5]

The demand for tickets throughout 1935 and 1936 had been so brisk that by the winter of 1936 it had also become necessary to expand the theatre. Capacity was increased from 300 to 433 seats by extending the auditorium laterally. The original 'village hall' design was making way for a proper theatre. Christie built a small balcony at the back, with his large box in the middle. This box was an ostentatious feature out of keeping with the simplicity of the rest of the auditorium. When Spike Hughes described it as 'a cross between a temple and a summer house'[6] he was undoubtedly right in feeling that it was a design more appropriate to the exterior.

Chauffeurs relaxing during a performance of Don Giovanni, *8 June 1939*

Opposite. *Looking along the Green Room towards the oriel window*

John Christie's sketch of his proposed box (right), based on a design by Edmond Warre, and the box in situ in the balcony, 1938 (left)

Opposite. Elevation and plan of the Opera House by Edmond Warre, showing the addition of the dressing rooms and Green Room. The Romanesque-style exterior cyclorama was never built

The addition of the balcony meant that part of what had previously been foyer space was lost, including the circular lily pond, an attraction which became a hazard when patrons occasionally fell in. These changes to the foyer created the opportunity to provide a Covered Way, allowing people to walk from the theatre to the Wallop dining halls in the dry.

A new dining hall with associated kitchen facilities was built on two levels, Middle and Over Wallop, following the incline of the hillside. Having sacrificed one ilex tree in 1935, John Christie could not be persuaded to fell another so soon. Thus the new restaurant was built round two trees, one ilex and one wych-elm. On 11 May 1937 *The Times* reported,

> It is proposed to fix a sword in one of them and give a free dinner to any Siegfried who can remove it; but Mr Christie guarantees that no Hunding will be present to spoil the banquets.

If Christie was not able to see works by his favourite composer performed in the theatre, he would introduce 'a little touch of Wagner' elsewhere at Glyndebourne. According to Christie there was evidence on site of another composer; while showing a journalist round the kitchen, he opened one of the vast refrigerators and announced as he did so, 'This is where we preserve Mozart.'[7]

People often ask why the restaurants are known as Nether, Middle and Over Wallop. They are named after the villages in Hampshire from which the Earls of Portsmouth take their family name. John Christie's

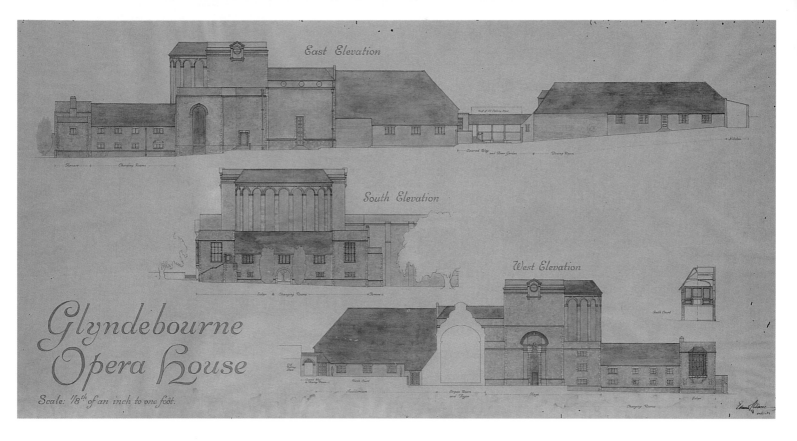

East Elevation

South Elevation

West Elevation

Glyndebourne
Opera House

Scale: 1/8th of an inch to one foot.

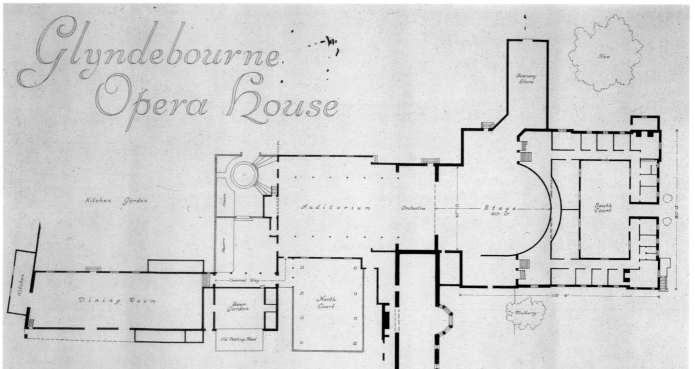

Glyndebourne
Opera House

Ilex

Scenery Store

Kitchen Garden

Auditorium *Orchestra* *Stage* *South Court*

Kitchen

Dining Room

Covered Way

Beer Garden

Old Potting Shed

North Court

Mulberry

Scale: 1/16th of an inch to one foot.

Edmund Warre
Architect.

The flytower under construction from the ha-ha lawn (left) and from the walled garden (opposite), 1938. In the foreground (left) are Fritz Busch, John Christie and Rudolf Bing with Tuppy, the Christie family pug dog

mother, Lady Rosamond Wallop, was a daughter of the 5th Earl of Portsmouth.

During the 1937 season, notwithstanding the improvements made to the size of the stage, there were complaints in the newspapers about the slowness of scene changes. This applied particularly to *Don Giovanni*, for which Hamish Wilson had designed elaborate sets that were a nightmare for the stage hands.

> Under the present arrangement the audience has a tedious wait, which they beguile by chattering, thus losing the thread of the music, while complicated manoeuvres with heavy pieces of structural woodwork are going on on the other side of the curtain.[8]

Christie refuted these criticisms, but underneath knew there was a need for change if the standard people had come to expect from

Glyndebourne was to be maintained. There was extra impetus for this work, because it had been decided to expand the repertory for the 1938 season to include Donizetti's *Don Pasquale* and the first professional production in England of Verdi's *Macbeth*, as well as three Mozart operas. For the first time an international name, Caspar Neher, had been engaged to design the costumes and sets for *Macbeth* and strong feelings were expressed by Rudolf Bing and Carl Ebert that such an important production would be seriously compromised if a flytower were not built. On 28 June 1937 Christie discussed the alterations with his business manager, Walter Edwards, who was a valued adviser on all his enterprises. Edwards noted in his diary that day:

> Mr Christie confirming that he had given up the proposal of removing the organ and throwing that end of the Music Room into the Theatre as a suggested extension, and that he had also given up the proposal to widen the proscenium opening. Further, that he was giving most careful consideration to the question of the proposed power structure over the stage, to enable the flying of scenery; that he was much concerned with the question of the appearance of such a structure. . .

Up to this point the buildings had retained a style and unity which a flytower, however stately the design, would destroy. The toughest test of the Christies' commitment to their enterprise had come and they knew there was no alternative but to proceed. The 'steel hat', as Christie called it, was designed by Every's of Lewes. It was some 50 feet long, 40 feet wide and 26 feet high, and the steel work used weighed 30 tons. It was covered with cedar shingles, an idea suggested by Walter Edwards, and there was a classical touch in the small wooden pilasters that decorated each side of the exterior. While it could in no way be described as an architectural asset, neither was it as unattractive as Christie had perhaps envisaged.

Christie's habit of changing his mind about alterations from time to time brought him into conflict with those around him. Between 1937 and 1938 he decided against installing two stage-lifts without telling key people such as Carl Ebert. Rudolf Bing wrote Christie a terse admonitory note:

> Ebert has informed me that he had not heard of your intention to cut out the lifts. Fortunately he has not relied on them for *Macbeth*. He has, however, worked out his producing idea for *Don Pasquale* on the basis of the new lifts . . . What would have happened if he and Neher had based their entire *Macbeth* production on the new lifts which were inserted in Neher's stage plan I don't know.[9]

A set design by Hamish Wilson for Don Pasquale, *1938, showing one of his characteristic staircases in the centre*

Opposite. A costume design for Macbeth *by Caspar Neher, who had previously worked with Carl Ebert at the Städtische Oper, Berlin, in the early 1930s*

Throwing plans into turmoil would have been unintentional on Christie's part. It was simply that the depth of his involvement and fascination with technical detail often made him forget the problems of artistic administration, particularly if his wife was not there to remind him.

While these alterations were in progress, Audrey was indeed taking a much needed rest at Villabassa in the Dolomites. On her own, without having to worry about her family, her responsibilities as hostess, or her singing, she had a chance to reflect:

> I then came down when it was practically dark & walked onto the little jetty & watched the changing lights & suddenly the hotel band struck up the 'Figaro' overture – it sounded enchanting across the water & from there seemed very well played . . . I was transported into that rather sultry atmosphere of our theatre at the start of 'Figaro' and suddenly came to in this rather rarified [*sic*] atmosphere to realize what an amazing thing we've done at Glybn. It is such a detached & different realization here – so far away.[10]

She sang two roles in the 1938 Festival – Norina in *Don Pasquale* and Susanna in *Le nozze di Figaro*.

Many of the bricklayers and painters employed on the alterations to the theatre were also delighted to be given their first on-stage roles as soldiers in Macbeth. Where else could local people have combined the duties of craftsmen during the day, actors in the evening and scene shifters at night?

Macbeth

Kosani: A
als Gmadlage

Helm

Leder im
Lang mir Metall
Keten

Leder
Koller

Keten-
handschuhe

Leder Stücke
mir Ketten

N 52

53

IN THE GROUNDS BETWEEN THE ACTS.

THE FOYER IS AN OPERATIC SETTING IN ITSELF.

THE NEW BALCONY AND THE SPECIAL GLYNDEBOURNE BOX.

AN ENTHUSIASTIC MOZART FESTIVAL AUDIENCE GIVE THE SINGERS AN OVATION AT EVERY PERFORMANCE

ON A FIRST NIGHT AT GLYNDEBOURNE, THE OPERA HOUSE SET IN THE HEART OF SUSSEX IN AN ENDEAVOUR "TO COMMAND SUCH

AID COUNTRY=HOUSE CHARMS.

THE TREE
GROWING THROUGH
THE DINING HALL RATHER
SUGGESTS THE FIRST ACT OF WAGNER'S 'VALKYRIE'

THE FINAL MOZARTIAN EFFECT:
GLYNEBOURNE IN THE LIGHT OF DEPARTING CARS.

ROYAN DE GERINFALL
GLYNDEBOURNE 1937.

'HAT THE WORLD WILL TURN TOWARDS ENGLAND."

Members of the first night audience in 1935
beside the lily pond. This was later replaced by a
covered way, as shown in the top left hand
corner of a spread from the Illustrated London
News of 1937

55

Top. *The famous 'gossip' chorus in Act III of Donizetti's* Don Pasquale, *1938*
Above. *The finale of Act I of* Don Giovanni, *1937, with Audrey Mildmay (Zerlina) and John Brownlee (Don Giovanni)*
Right. *Malcolm and Macduff beside the fallen Macbeth. The sizeable cast of extras for Verdi's* Macbeth, *1938, included many of John Christie's employees*

Jock Gough, *chief stage*
technician, on stage inspecting
one of the lighting bars and
holding the Christie family pug
dog in his arms (right) *and*
drawn by Kenneth Green shortly
before he retired from
Glyndebourne in 1963 (above)

Rudolf Bing studying costume
designs with wardrobe mistress,
Juliette Magny, 1938

Only one season remained before world events destroyed this special local intimacy. Throughout the summer of 1939 Christie refused to be downcast by the worsening international situation. Plans for the 1940 season went ahead, and a preliminary leaflet was prepared including *Carmen* among the operas to be staged that year. It was not to happen. On 19 July 1940 Audrey Christie, with her two children, Rosamond and George, set sail for Canada, a place of safety during a war they hoped would soon be over. It was a harsh existence beset by financial difficulties; stringent currency regulations meant that John Christie was unable to send them any money, and on occasion Audrey was literally forced to sing for their suppers. They were not able to return to England until May 1944.

Christie was lonely and unhappy without his family. At first he spent a good deal of time at Tapeley, but by the early summer of 1941 he was back at Glyndebourne, where there was more to occupy his attention. He was surrounded by 100 evacuee children who ran in the long grass that was once lawn, through the vegetable garden that was once a rose garden, played in the Green Room and slept in the artists' dressing rooms.

In the theatre Christie continued to make improvements, with the assistance of his Chief Technician Jock Gough, a short, strong-minded, very individual Scotsman. Christie first met him when Jock was employed as a stage carpenter at Tunbridge Wells Opera House. They immediately developed a rapport and respect for each other, which strengthened when Christie asked him to come and work in his new opera house at Glyndebourne. From late 1941 until early 1942, with advice from Bernard Sharp and Bill Thorpe, they spent days enlarging the roof chamber above the auditorium and upgrading the lighting it contained.

Larger projects in the theatre and its outbuildings were impossible because of a lack of labour and materials. Indeed, for some time after the war it looked as if six seasons might be the sum total of Glyndebourne's operatic output.

Audrey Christie with her children Rosamond and George

Evacuee children in the Green Room during the Second World War

59

Osbert Lancaster's view of the Glyndebourne scene, used as the programme book cover in 1960. On the left hand side John Christie is seen with his pug dog. To his left the General Administrator, Moran Caplat, stands talking to the conductor, Vittorio Gui. On the far right are Jock Gough and Frank Harvey, the Head Gardener, who in reality rarely spoke to each other

5

The gardens

'The gardens are an intimate and essential part of the whole.'
John Christie, interview for the BBC, 1957[1]

RUNNING PARALLEL with the improvements to the house and the addition of the Organ Room and opera house was the development of the Glyndebourne gardens. From Victorian times until John Christie took up residence in 1913, there had been a single terrace by the house and a small ha-ha lawn with parkland beyond. A large area at the back was used as an orchard and kitchen garden, and this was where Christie later sited the opera house. Around the turn of the century, a beautiful double avenue of trees was planted in the field opposite the house, leading from an area known as The Vinegars down to the road; but it seems to have had a short life and may possibly have been felled for timber during the First World War. The Vinegars supposedly acquired that name in the seventeenth century after vines had been planted there which produced wine of such poor quality that it tasted like vinegar. It is an entertaining story, but no documentary evidence or bottles of wine lingering in the Christie cellars have been found to support it. Another area with a memorable name is 'Old Hag' to the north of the house, which became increasingly wooded in Victorian times as pheasant shooting grew in popularity. 'Hag' is the name for rings of fungus supposedly left by the fairies.

As with all his projects, Christie's plans for the garden were ambitious. By 1920 he was employing a head gardener and four assistants to sow the lawns, clear the ponds, dig out a new reservoir, extend the terrace and grow grapes, peaches, nectarines and tomatoes in his hot houses. Until 1924 he had difficulty in finding a head gardener who could cope with his constant flow of new ideas which he expected to be carried out with great speed. That year Frank Harvey came for an interview. It was short and to the point:

'I do not want a Victorian gardener. Can you grow grapes?'
'Yes, Sir.'
'Can you grow peas and celery?'
'Yes, Sir.'
'Very well. You are engaged.'[2]

A stroll by the pond, 1957

A pastel of the Urn Garden in high summer by Peter Thomas

Opposite. *Looking through the Irish yews to the Urn Garden and Lawn Hill beyond*

Like Jock Gough, the Chief Technician, Harvey was a strong character who was prepared to stand his ground and quash some of Christie's more extravagant ideas. There is a tale of his doing battle with Edmond Warre over a summer house. Warre wanted to position it in the exact place where Harvey had just laboriously opened up a view of the Downs; Harvey refused to allow it and eventually he won.

Under Harvey the gardens flourished. All those who remember them in the 1930s regard that period as their peak. It was then possible to walk round all three ponds; the herbaceous borders were outstanding; and the backstage buildings and rehearsal rooms had not yet seriously encroached on the garden. The latter point was not one with which Audrey Christie agreed. In 1932 she wrote to her husband,

> Darling, I knew you'd go on covering up all the available soil with buildings at home. I hope the new lavatories won't kill the lilies of the valley – although you dislike them I love them! If they have to be moved they might be tucked away out of vision in the sweet little dell beyond the ilexes![3]

After her death in 1953 John Christie ensured that her presence was remembered in the gardens by making the 'little dell beyond the ilexes'

into the Audrey Mildmay Memorial Garden. While she was still alive Audrey Christie took a keen interest in the garden. She gratefully accepted horticultural advice from her mother-in-law, something which her husband had never been prepared to do. In fact, Lady Rosamond was acknowledged to have created a very fine garden at her home at Tapeley.

To the artists and staff engaged for the Opera Festivals the gardens were, and are, a very special part of Glyndebourne. In the 1930s, with no other space available, some rehearsals took place outside. There was at that time a boat and boathouse at the top of the first pond, and between rehearsals artists gently floated among the water lilies, swans and flamingoes. It was an idyllic setting that inspired many of them to attain greater heights on stage.

> I remember John Christie once saying 'Well you see the nature of the place has something to do with it. Imagine if you were looking out of your window and there was flat country as far as you could see and at the very end of the horizon there was a gate, well, that's alright, but what can it do to your spirit?'[4]

Frank Harvey watering the herbaceous borders in the Walled Garden, and a view across the lawn to the house, 1938

The orchestra derived particular pleasure from the croquet lawn, playing their special version of the game while the audience dined in the long interval. Picnicking became increasingly popular from the 1950s onwards. At first, people had a tendency to stay close to their cars, but later they spread to all corners of the gardens, some positioning themselves near the Green Room to hear the artists warm up before the second half while others preferred to sit near the pond.

Each member of the audience had a favourite area, whether it was the sunken garden at the top of the first pond, noted for its irises, the rose garden (now the Urn Garden) planted with roses and Mrs Simkins pinks which perfumed the evening air, or the ha-ha lawn with its views of the Downs. What everyone appreciated then, as now, is the comfortable blend of formality and informality.

Designs influenced by the Glyndebourne setting

Above. *Watercolour by Sir Hugh Casson for the Glyndebourne programme book cover, 1979*

Right. *Design by William Dudley for* Die Entführung aus dem Serail, *1980. Based on the view of Glyndebourne from beyond the ha-ha, the house, flytower, Green Room and rehearsal stage all acquire domes and the ha-ha becomes a river carrying feluccas*

Opposite. *A picnic scene by Lila de Nobili, 1961*

*Benjamin Britten, Eric Crozier (producer) and
Ernest Ansermet, seated, with the singers
Otakar Kraus, Kathleen Ferrier, Peter Pears
and Nancy Evans in the gardens during
rehearsals of Britten's opera* The Rape of
Lucretia *in 1946*

6

Reawakening

'As I stood in the empty Opera Theatre I couldn't help feeling that the place wasn't dead but just sleeping, and that at a given signal the covers would be whisked off the stalls, the house lights would go down, the stage and orchestra pit would fill with artists eager once more to pick up the threads, which this miserable war has severed, and begin the happy work of preparing for another of those memorable seasons.'[1]

(Ralph Nicholson in a letter to John Christie, October 1944)

THE FIRST EVENT in the theatre after the war, a Welcome Home Concert on 17 June 1945, was of necessity 'low key' in comparison with the operatic triumphs that had gone before. However, the calibre of the artists was in no way diminished: Irene Eisinger, Dino Borgioli, Roy Henderson and David Franklin sang arias from their Glyndebourne repertoire accompanied by the Philharmonic String Trio. But after that there was a silence which threatened to persist. The post-war economic situation was such that John Christie could no longer afford to finance an opera festival. Without an alternative source of private funding or a government grant, Glyndebourne's future as an international opera venue seemed doomed.

In the absence of an audience, Christie had already found an alternative use for some of the buildings. Urgent messages were sent to the Devon estate office asking them to purchase old fishing nets. When these arrived, Mildmay dining hall and the waiters' dormitories (known as the Plashetts after the Plashett Estate owned by Christie between Ringmer and Uckfield) were turned into indoor cricket nets. George Christie remembers his father bowling low, fast balls at him and being delighted when they were damaged beyond repair after hitting radiators – this presumably being an indication of his son's improving abilities as a batsman.[2]

Fortunately the General Manager, Rudolf Bing, was not to be deterred from finding a proper use for the theatre and its outbuildings. He began negotiations with Benjamin Britten, Peter Pears and Eric Crozier, which were to lead to the world premieres of *The Rape of Lucretia* and *Albert Herring* at Glyndebourne in 1946 and 1947. However, during the summers of 1948 and 1949 there were only short concert seasons in the opera

GLYNDEBOURNE
OPERA HOUSE

Sunday, June 17, 1945
AT 3 P.M.

WELCOME HOME
CONCERT

BY

GLYNDEBOURNE ARTISTS

IRENE EISINGER
DINO BORGIOLI
ROY HENDERSON
DAVID FRANKLIN
THE PHILHARMONIC STRING TRIO
(DAVID MARTIN, MAX GILBERT, JAMES WHITEHEAD)

THE PROGRAMME WILL INCLUDE
MUSIC FROM THEIR
GLYNDEBOURNE REPERTOIRE

COLLECTION IN AID OF THE RINGMER
WELCOME-HOME FUND

After the war, 17 June 1945

Above left. *Design by Rolf Gérard for the 1950 production of* Die Entführung aus dem Serail *one of two Mozart operas which made up the first post war season*

Above right. *Oliver Messel's design for Susanna in* Le nozze di Figaro, *1955*

house. Glyndebourne's real work continued at Edinburgh where in 1947 the Christies and Rudolf Bing had helped to found the annual Festival. Glyndebourne performed there with financial assistance from the Edinburgh Festival Society while in Sussex the desperate search continued for a means of re-starting the summer Festival.

Rescue came from John Spedan Lewis of the John Lewis Partnership, a close friend of the Christies and loyal supporter of Glyndebourne since its inception. He gave the sum of £12,500, which enabled the Festival to recommence in 1950 with a fourteen-performance season of Mozart operas, seven of *Die Entführung* and seven of *Così fan tutte*.

Much activity was required to bring Glyndebourne back to life, a process made more difficult by the continuing rationing of such basic commodities as petrol to mow the lawns. Jack Brymer remembers the gardens being very neglected and the buildings feeling dismal and dank for two or three years before the old Glyndebourne atmosphere returned.[3]

But John Christie had lost none of his enthusiasm for the detail of the building. The acoustician Hope Bagenal described a visit to Glyndebourne in March 1950:

Next morning we went over the theatre. He [John Christie] has a factotum called Gough – 'the best stage hand in Europe' who looks after him – and wherever they are in the theatre they talk to each other through floors and ceilings and trap doors. Christie *explained* to me bits of machinery – but the explanation was the harder to understand of the two. We went through all the dressing rooms specially built round a little courtyard giving on to the garden. . . . In the wardrobe were large plywood trunks labelled 'Figaro' or 'Cosi fan'. Every dressing room has a shower and WCs wide enough to take crinolines, 'just think of the *idiots* who built Sadler's Wells not *knowing* that WCs ought to take crinolines.'[4]

The Street Scene, Act I Scene 2 of Don Giovanni, *designed by John Piper, 1951*

By autumn 1950 Christie had instructed a young architect called Leslie Fairweather to draw up plans for extending the auditorium. These resulted in Christie's imposing balcony box being removed – for two years he used a box at the back of the stalls – and the addition of a number of seats in the balcony which brought the theatre capacity to 592. This was the first of three major alterations to the theatre during the 1950s.

In 1951 Miki Sekers, a charismatic Hungarian entrepreneur who owned West Cumberland Silk Mills, gave all the materials for the *Don Giovanni* costumes. He also suggested that a Glyndebourne Festival Society should be established to which individual and corporate members

Moran Caplat, Jock Gough and John Christie discussing structural alterations to the theatre, winter 1951

Above right. *George Foa and Carl Ebert planning the BBC television transmission of* Die Entführung aus dem Serail, *1953*

would pay an annual subscription in return for two and four complimentary seats respectively and a copy of the programme book. The creation of the programme book was a further funding idea which he hoped would raise £20,000 by attracting forty advertisers at the rate of £500 per page (a sum the equivalent of just over £8,000 today). In the event, the programme book attracted a creditable eighteen advertisers. Both these schemes were barely fledged – the Festival Society was officially founded in November 1951 and the first programme book published in 1952 – when, over the winter of 1952/53, John Christie embarked on the second of his three major alterations to the theatre, a complete restructuring of the auditorium. At that time Glyndebourne's financial uncertainties were coupled with grave difficulties in obtaining licences for any sort of structural work. Once again, Glyndebourne showed that willingness to take risks which had been its hallmark from the beginning.

Ringmer Building Works were engaged to widen the auditorium and, as a result, the proscenium was also enlarged to maintain sight-lines. In addition, the barrel-vaulted auditorium ceiling was rebuilt and replaced with what has been described as a 'hyperbolic parabola'.[5] Many felt the acoustic was adversely affected; and years of experimentation followed with acoustic panels and raising and lowering the height of the orchestra pit. After alterations to deepen the pit in 1964, a number of the orchestra players were unhappy:

Things like the *Traviata* solo that heartbreaking solo of a clarinet, you had to play it almost mezzo-forte instead of a withdrawn pianissimo which it should be. It should almost be at the back of the mind; it should be something inhibited.[6]

The total cost of the alterations came to £8,825; Christie took great delight in informing David Eccles at the Ministry of Works that *his* firm had managed to do the work so economically that it had cost £1,195 less than the permit granted for £10,000.

As always the work force was closely supervised by Christie himself and Jock Gough. The two often argued fiercely about how certain aspects of the building work should be executed, and Gough nearly always won. Jock was a very talented technician, 'a great man of the theatre'[7] and a 'dictator'[8] in matters to do with the stage. On being presented with a complicated set design or plan to alter part of the opera house, his first response was 'It can't be done.'[9] If he felt particularly pressurized by Carl Ebert or one of the designers, he would throw down his cap, 'resign' and stomp off. Usually he would appear for work the next day as if nothing had happened. When, in his view, the fracas had been more serious it would take the combined efforts of a home visit from John Christie and Carl Ebert to persuade him to return. He would then devise some ingenious method of achieving the impossible – making the scenery fit on stage or creating a piece of equipment to give just the required effect.

Carl Ebert and John Christie sharing a joke in the late 1950s

Fritz Busch, John Christie and Carl Ebert, 1951

Magic evening at Glyndebourne by Beryl Cook, 1991

The audience in 1969. Cover for the Glyndebourne programme book, designed by Osbert Lancaster. George and Mary Christie, with two of their children, are seated in the second box from the right behind the stalls. Moran Caplat is in the top left-hand box

John Christie and Jock Gough surveying alterations to the auditorium roof space, 1952

Christie thrived on these turbulent winters. Moran Caplat remembers him being happier when he had the challenge of solving the intricate problems thrown up by the building alterations than when everything was running smoothly during the Festival. This is supported by his idiosyncratic forewords to the programme books throughout the 1950s which focus on building alterations, funding for the arts and the ideals on which Glyndebourne's work is based ('We should aim at the sky, but have our feet on the ground'[10]), but make little detailed reference to the operas performed on stage.

In 1957 the theatre underwent its third major change when once again the auditorium ceiling was completely rebuilt. Hope Bagenal had recommended that in order to improve the sound there should be no large, unbroken, flat surfaces anywhere in the theatre. It was at this point that the three protruding beams alternating with flat recesses became a feature of the theatre ceiling that was to remain until the end.

Every alteration to the theatre involved the addition of a few more seats. The visibility of the stage from these seats was a major preoccupation of Christie's. He insisted on sitting in all of them before allowing them to be screwed down to the floor. Any complaints about sight-lines were answered by Christie himself. One about the view from new seats in the balcony received this response:

> The back three rows of the balcony are, I think, the ones concerned. The front one of the three we cannot alter, owing to the difficulty which would arise from steps and fire regulations. But the back two we have altered, and according to 'Jock' who of course controls everything here – assisted by the pug dog 'Sock' – we have solved your problem satisfactorily.[11]

The phrase about Jock and Sock's control of Glyndebourne was a favourite of John Christie's. As we have seen, Jock did indeed have great influence. After the tragic death of Audrey Christie in 1953 at the early age of 52, it was Jock who took over her role of taming Christie's wilder flights of fancy for his theatre.

The rehearsal stage was built in 1959. Leslie Fairweather remembers John Christie telephoning him late one Friday night and telling him that he had decided to build a rehearsal stage, and the men [from Ringmer Building Works] were ready to start on Monday morning. Could Fairweather draw up some plans? Early on Monday morning Fairweather took his plans, which had been approved by Christie over the weekend, to the Lewes building surveyors, who exploded with fury because they knew nothing about the project. This was quite typical of Christie, who had a complete disregard for planning rules and regulations. By the time Fairweather arrived at Glyndebourne that day, the men were already digging out the foundations.

In fact the rehearsal stage was an idea first mooted in 1953. It enabled one opera to be in rehearsal or performance on the main stage and, at the same time, another to be on the rehearsal stage. The size of the latter was similar to, and on the same level as, the main stage, thus making it possible to rehearse an opera with full scenery by sliding the sets from the stage or backstage areas into the room and closing a sound-proof door.

The building itself was a square block constructed of the familiar brick-and-sandstone, 'plum pudding', mixture to tone with the Green Room and dressing room block next to it. There was one departure from its utilitarian nature – a grandiose double flight of stairs which were a whim of John Christie's, distinctly out of keeping with the rest of the design.

It was the last major addition to the theatre during Christie's lifetime. In the 1962 programme book he wrote:

> I see no sign of weakness except that Sock, the Pug Dog, who is in control of course, is getting older and may not be able to carry out large operations which belong to the future.

Perhaps this was the way he was feeling himself, for on 4 July 1962, shortly before the evening's performance of *Così fan tutte*, he died at the age of 79.

Roofing the balcony extension, 1953

The 'theatrical' approach to the rehearsal stage, 1959

7

A *new vision*

'A state without the means of some change is without the means of its conservation.'[1]

Almost inevitably after the death of such a powerful figure, Glyndebourne suffered a loss of direction. One of the ways in which the General Manager, Moran Caplat, encouraged Glyndebourne itself to take on a more positive role was by making it a permanent administrative base for the opera. Until 1963, members of the staff had worked at Glyndebourne during the Festival and in London, at offices in Baker Street, for the rest of the year. When the lease on Baker Street ran out and negotiations to rent space in another rather appropriate London venue – the house where Mozart stayed in Ebury Street – fell through, a row of staff boxes with office accommodation backing onto them was added to the theatre at balcony level on each side of the auditorium. Glyndebourne was thus able to function on home ground for twelve months of the year rather than four.

In general, although alterations continued – converting garages, stables and other domestic outbuildings into rehearsal rooms, offices and scenery stores was a much favoured winter activity – projects on a 'John Christie scale' ceased. The main reason for this was financial. Throughout the early 1960s Glyndebourne Productions had suffered a steadily increasing deficit because of the declining value of box office income relative to the escalating costs of running a high-class opera house.

Eventually, a major appeal was launched in 1964 to help provide funds for a new transistorized lighting control system (to replace the Bordoni in use since 1934), and for the permanent office accommodation already mentioned as well as other general maintenance and repairs. A year later £64,064 had been raised, but the work had cost £93,313. This kind of financial imbalance continued until the mid-1970s when George Christie, who had gradually taken a stronger role as Chairman, realized that unless a larger proportion of income could be raised by sponsorship Glyndebourne would cease to exist. He was valuably assisted in seeking sponsors by Sir Alex Alexander, then Chairman of Imperial Food, who,

Britten's A Midsummer Night's Dream, *designed by John and Elizabeth Bury, 1981.* Above *Design for a tree person and* (opposite) *Oberon and Puck plotting mischief in the forest*

81

Above right. The director Trevor Nunn and his assistant, Alby James, rehearsing Damon Evans, Bruce Hubbard, Willard White and Richie Pitts for Porgy and Bess, 1987, *in the Lily Davis Room, which is seen to the right of the photograph* above

like Glyndebourne's first major fund-raiser, Miki Sekers, was of Central European descent. From then onwards a wide range of well-known corporate bodies have supported the Opera Festival financially and played an essential role in its survival.

Generous donations also enabled Glyndebourne to continue adding to and altering the motley array of outbuildings which are necessary to service any large opera company. In 1971 Henry Davis gave £15,000 in memory of his wife, Lily; this sum, together with £7,500 given by The Pilgrim Trust, was used to build a large new rehearsal room – the Lily Davis Room – in close proximity to the stage. 'Plum pudding' brickwork was abandoned in favour of a plain brick, copper-clad building with full-length windows overlooking the Downs and a little balcony much used for watching tennis matches between singers, conductors and administrative staff.

In 1979 the family of the late Charles Turton gave £25,000 towards the conversion and extension of a rehearsal room complex, called 'Tuff Turton' in his memory.

It has to be said that the rehearsal stage was the last old Glyndebourne building to have any sense of style. Subsequent developments were functional but undistinguished. In addition to financial constraints, there would seem to be two main reasons for this: firstly, for many years after

John Christie's death no one took the same all-consuming interest in the building work, therefore the results became less sympathetic to their surroundings. Secondly, many of John Christie's other businesses which had acted as a 'support system' in building different parts of the opera house had been dispersed – for example, the Plashett Estate, which had provided timber for simple but stylish doors and floors had been sold in 1965.

In 1982 Glyndebourne's 50th Birthday Appeal was launched with the principal aim of improving facilities backstage. Increasingly complex set designs demanded more space, both for storage and for safety and efficiency. By October 1983 the appeal had raised over £625,000. A new scene dock was built to designs by Ford, Newman and Whitty, which involved the felling of another of John Christie's favourite ilex trees. Newman and Whitty became architects to Glyndebourne in 1966, when even John Christie might have conceded that the growing number of planning rules

Cramped backstage storage facilities, 1991

Rehearsing Il ritorno d'Ulisse in patria, *1972, one of the productions that tested the capacity of the stage machinery to its limits*

Evening sunlight on the lawns, the last season in the old Opera House, 1992

and regulations dictated the involvement of a professional company in all Glyndebourne's alterations. The scene dock was a plain brick building which marked the last big change to the old theatre.

Throughout the 1980s, opera became an increasingly popular art form. Ticket demand was unprecedented and public expectation of performers and performances reached a peak. Glyndebourne simply could not keep pace with the applications for seats. On-stage standards continued to be very high, but there was a growing awareness that the theatre's facilities were being stretched to the limit in order to achieve those standards. How was Glyndebourne to maintain its position and ensure its survival?

84

Any major refurbishment of the existing theatre would be seriously compromised by its location next to the Organ Room, which together with the main house is a listed building. It would also be compromised by the desire to retain the Green Room and dressing-room block which limited further extensions backstage. Most important of all, the auditorium could not be made larger without losing the sense of intimacy which was its greatest asset.

Gradually George Christie realized that the only solution was to build a completely new opera house. It is a vision of which his father would have been proud, and in his idealistic way he would have said, 'Do the best you can because I want to give my country a model of perfection.'[2]

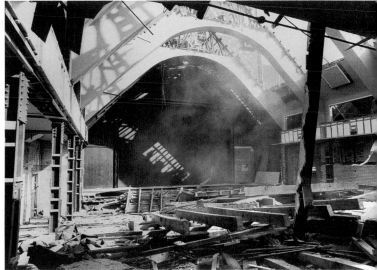

Glyndebourne old and new

Left. *The audience at the final performance in the old theatre. A Gala Concert in the presence of HRH The Prince of Wales on 24 July 1992*

The old auditorium during demolition, 6 August 1992 (top) and the emerging semicircular shape of the backstage area with the Lily Davis rehearsal room, old flytower and Organ Room in the background

The commission

GEORGE CHRISTIE announced his idea for a new theatre in the 1987 Festival programme. 'The idea is merely a glint in my eye . . . which could not conceivably materialise in less than half-a-dozen years, if ever. Were it to happen it would not – indeed, must not – on any account be undertaken on a scale such as to destroy the intimacy of the present theatre.'

The underlying cause, he explained, was a 'deepening anxiety arising from the relentless and voracious quest for tickets . . . It is good to be wanted; but there is a point when, if you can't respond to the demand, you are at risk of creating needless chagrin and disenchantment. In the final analysis the only way out is to have a bigger auditorium.'

The limiting factor in the old theatre was the proscenium arch. 'We cannot make it any wider within the present roof structure and without knocking down the Organ Room – and this I refuse to do,' Christie wrote in December 1987.

His first step was to commission a feasibility study from John Bury, the theatre designer and consultant who had designed a series of Glyndebourne productions for Peter Hall, including *Le nozze di Figaro*, *Fidelio* and *Carmen*. 'He did a first cockshy in the form of a fan which proved it was possible to get 1,200 seats on the footprint of the old theatre – none of them further back than in the existing theatre.'

Bury also provided the crucial initial steer on the width of the new proscenium arch. It had to be wide enough to provide good sight-lines from the enlarged auditorium – but make it too large and the costs of staging productions would increase disproportionately, and it would lose that theatrical imperative – intimacy.

Bury explains that 'the proscenium arch is the measure of the building. From its dimensions, everything else follows – the stage, the wing space, the height of the flytower. It's a formula. You don't have to follow it but it's useful.' He adds, 'The key sight-line is how much of the backstage you can see. I say it should be at least 4 metres of the backcloth for everyone. That's an 8-foot giant on a 6-foot rostrum.'

John Bury produced a plan which he described as having been 'laid out on those principles established in the planning stages of the

Early stages of construction work on the auditorium, October 1992. In the background is the old dressing-room block now converted into offices and rehearsal rooms

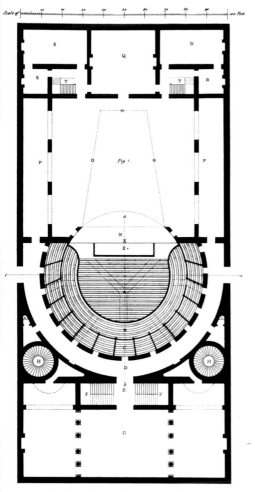

Design for a theatre with a circular auditorium by George Saunders in A Treatise on Theatres, *1790*

Edinburgh Opera House, *i.e.*, not too wide a fan, a trumpet-shaped auditorium, as large a clear volume as possible with shallow balconies without too much overhang and not too considerable a rake to the stalls. Golden rule: all seats should be able to see the ceiling cove above the orchestra pit.'

George Christie now turned for practical guidance to the property developer Stuart Lipton. 'He helped us look at a cross section of architects from classical to modern. We drew up a short list of twelve, and nine came to be interviewed. I said we'd limit ourselves to British architects, not because I'm saying they're better, but because there are a lot of good ones around.'

In August 1988 he sent the nine architects what he called his 'idle thoughts'. 'Glyndebourne', he said, 'is a country house which has bred an opera house. There is emphatically no need in rebuilding the theatre to be slavish to the style of the house; and there is, even more emphatically, no need to be slavish to the existing theatre which has grown piecemeal over the last 50-odd years and which is architecturally a complete hybrid (witness the framed exhibition of the original design as envisaged by my father and his architect).'

Secondly, he said he was seeking for a theatre design which aesthetically persuaded the audience of its justification and 'which convinces all of us using it (both backstage and front-of-house) of its practicability.' And he added pointedly, 'It can be controversial to a point that does not alienate the majority.'

His third idle thought was ultimately to become the key to the whole design. 'I recognize that any good piece of architecture must make a "statement", but the style which comes from that statement has got to convince in the first year of the building's existence as well as for the next 100 years.' He was looking 'for something that would neither provoke violent reactions nor be depressingly reactionary.'

Then came his own assessment of the existing theatre, with the bluntness that only extreme familiarity can bring: a theatre which 'is in quite large measure of such architectural indifference that only improvement can happen – hence the free passage which English Heritage has given us.'

The twinkle in George Christie's eye, and by now it was much more than that, had above all to be a piece of architecture. This in itself is of importance, for in Britain, and indeed elsewhere, theatres have relatively rarely been designed by leading architects. The main exceptions occurred in the years around 1800 when Henry Holland, Benjamin Dean Wyatt and Sir Robert Smirke designed a series of beautiful theatres. To this can be added E. M. Barry's Covent Garden Opera House.

Yet these are few when compared to the output of the theatre specialists. Frank Matcham designed over 160 theatres. C. J. Phipps did 60. In Europe the famous pair Fellner and Helmer designed 165 theatres from Barcelona to Odessa, between 1870 and 1910. In the United States, J. B. MacElfatrick built over 250, and a generation later Thomas Lamb designed some 250 theatres and cinemas.

Most theatres were designed by theatre specialists. Matcham, genius though he certainly was, was not even an architect, and designed little else bar two town halls and a ballroom. As far as the architectural profession was concerned, theatre design was considered more a branch of entertainment than architecture – like pubs.

George Christie's nine architects are all leading figures at particular points of the architecture spectrum. Robert Adam has made a name for classical buildings. Peter Ahrends is a much respected modernist. Edward Cullinan has developed a distinctive brand of contemporary vernacular – highly responsive to local materials and traditions. Norman Foster is the apostle of high tech. Michael and Patty Hopkins have taken functionalism down a new contextual road. Sam Lloyd provides sensitive design in historic settings. Richard MacCormac has made modernism altogether more friendly and less anonymous. The late James Stirling, in partnership with Michael Wilford, was the most famous British exponent of Post-Modernism. Nicholas Thompson, from Renton Howard Wood Levine, represented the practice with the widest theatre experience in Britain, with numerous successful restorations and rebuildings to its credit.

Christie enlarges on what he considered the key requirements: 'First the shape of the flytower. I said that's something that will be architecturally very evident. It must be given a form acceptable to everybody.'

Second, he says, was 'the feel of the auditorium. What it's going to be dressed in. It's got to be hugely welcoming. Timber-clad, not plush gilt or velvet. It has to be both functional and friendly.'

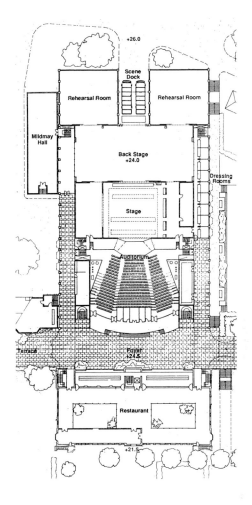

John Bury's initial fan-shaped plan designed to show how an auditorium seating over 1,000 people could be created without anyone sitting further from the stage than in the old theatre

91

His next point was 'an effect once considered impossible, namely a marriage of flattering resonance and absolute clarity, where every single voice and instrument can be heard.'

Another of his thoughts concerned lighting: 'I wanted lots of light sources. I was deeply anxious not to have uniformity. I wanted atmosphere and this meant low voltage – but enough light for people to read their programmes, especially in the body of the auditorium where there is no immediate light.'

Individual architects came up with intriguing ideas. MacCormac placed an emphasis on creating a sense of occasion and arrival. Cullinan suggested a restaurant on top of the flytower, not only to take advantage of the view, but to make it architecturally more attractive.

Glyndebourne had said it would select a short list of up to three architects. In the event, just two were chosen: Michael Hopkins and James Stirling. 'Each had three months to provide two-dimensional concepts and models,' says Christie. To make the task worthwhile they were offered £20,000 – though Christie, ever mindful of Glyndebourne's hard-won pennies, added that the winner would have the £20,000 deducted from his fee if the theatre proceeded. He explains, 'For all the ambitious plans, the maximum that Glyndebourne was committed to at this stage was £40,000.'

Both architects proposed to build on or near the old theatre. Christie liked the Stirling design, 'but it created a degree of sprawl which I was anxious to avoid. By contrast, Michael Hopkins's design was on the footprint of the old theatre, though bigger. This appealed to me. I didn't want a village at Glyndebourne, but one clearly defined edifice.'

Christie says that it would have been easier to go for Stirling in many ways. 'We could have continued in the old theatre while building the new one, as his was next door. He also suggested converting the old theatre to various uses – though these were never finally worked out.'

The Stirling and Wilford design had one other big advantage – foyers with direct access to the gardens. For Glyndebourne, they developed the long single-storey loggias they had used at the Performing Arts Center at Cornell University in New York State. Against this, Hopkins proposed a buffer between the new opera house and the garden – in the form of the old dressing-room block. Stirling's appealing features were not enough to swing Christie against the Hopkinses' strong statement.

The design which won the commission for Michael and Patty Hopkins was decidedly different from the theatre they have built. At that stage, the opera house was rectangular – taking its shape from the fan-shaped auditorium that John Bury had set out.

Intriguingly, it was Bury who presaged a different course as early as 1987. In a letter of 3 July to Brian Dickie, then Glyndebourne's general administrator, he wrote, 'I must admit I am still very worried about 1,150 people on a continuous rake with no overhangs. If that is built to GLC specifications one ends up with the Olivier. My thinking at this stage is that if we are building an opera house it should be one. Not in stucco, no cherubs, but in wood if they will let us and on the German Hof Theater format. Boxes with loose chairs and everybody squeezed into as small a volume as possible. Tradition without the pastiche! A Mozart House for Mozart operas. Not another geometric barn.'

Below left. *Eric Gabriel, Project Manager, Anthony Whitworth-Jones, General Director and Patty Hopkins studying plans for the new theatre, 1991*

Below. *John Bury (centre), theatre consultant, with Michael Hopkins* (left) *and George Christie at a Client Steering Group meeting, December 1991*

Aerial view of the Hopkins model. The remarkable geometric precision of the design is immediately evident in the roofs

George Christie and Michael Hopkins looking into the model of the auditorium, January 1992

9

The design

GEORGE CHRISTIE had chosen an architect not a design – or, as he and his wife Mary became increasingly aware, they had two architects, for Michael and Patty Hopkins are a husband-and-wife team to an extent rare in architecture – as confirmed in February 1994 when the RIBA's annual gold medal was awarded to them jointly. With them came a flourishing and highly professional practice, including other partners of outstanding ability in their own right. Robin Snell, an associate in the practice, was to become the project architect whose time was almost totally devoted to the building of the new opera house from September 1989 to the opening night.

For everyone involved there were three overriding objectives – intimacy, good sight-lines and superb acoustics – coupled with on-stage and backstage facilities of an altogether new order. The need now was to bring in professional theatre consultants and acousticians. With Michael and Patty Hopkins, George Christie selected Theatre Projects Consultants and Arup Acoustics.

Iain Mackintosh of Theatre Projects brought a new element into the project: an unrivalled historical knowledge of older theatres and opera houses, in terms not only of their design and evolution, but of their actual theatrical quality – whether for actors, singers, directors or producers. With a group of fellow enthusiasts, he had researched and staged in 1982 a remarkable exhibition, *Curtains!!!*, documenting every surviving theatre in Britain whether in or out of use. Thanks to their enthusiasm, many of these theatres, even long disused ones, have subsequently been restored and reopened.

Breathing life into historic theatres is only one half of the company's work; in North America, even more than in Britain, they are involved in creating some of the most advanced new theatres of recent years. Alan Russell, the partner responsible for stage engineering and stage lighting at Glyndebourne, played a key role at the Barbican for the Royal Shakespeare Company, worked on the renovation of the Teatro Colón in Buenos Aires, and most recently on the remarkable auditorium at Cerritos in Los Angeles, which can change overnight from a 900-seat drama theatre into a 2,000-seat concert hall.

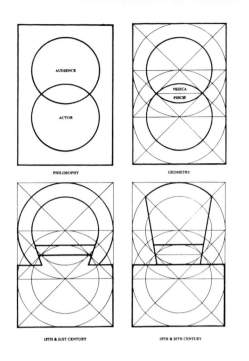

Iain Mackintosh's diagram from his book Architecture, Actor and Audience *(1993), showing the interlocking worlds of the stage and the auditorium through the centuries. The fish-shaped area where the circles overlap is known as the* vesica piscis

An early drawing from April 1990 by Theatre Projects Consultants illustrating the horseshoe auditorium set out according to sacred ad quadratum *geometry. The area of power, the* vesica piscis, *is occupied by singer, orchestra and conductor*

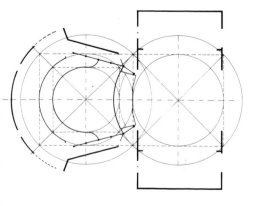

Iain Mackintosh had thought long and carefully about building an opera house of traditional form. Christie acknowledges that it was Mackintosh 'who convinced everybody that the horseshoe was the best shape. It happened remarkably quickly. We all felt that intimacy would be most easily achieved with the people in the audience wrapped round like wallpaper. That's something that neither the fan shape nor the shoebox does.'

Mackintosh poses the basic paradox between a fan shape and a horseshoe: 'People don't realize that a theatre where every seat has excellent sight-lines is not a good theatre. A good theatre invariably has some seats with bad sight-lines.' The fan shape, he argues, may be suitable for cinemas, but it is not appropriate for opera houses where the audience, and the sense of occasion that comes with it, are essential to the spectacle and the excitement. To support his point, Mackintosh quotes a 1767 *Treatise on Opera* by Count Algarotti, who suggested architects should 'contrive that the audience may form part of the spectacle to each other, ranged as books in a library.'

Here Mackintosh saw a unique opportunity. 'At Glyndebourne there is a specific requirement for staff seats. For once you have justified bad sight-lines. The staff need to be close to the stage so the management can see the singers, but they don't need a view of the whole stage, which they know only too well from rehearsals. Side seats close to the stage are particularly apposite, as management can slip swiftly and quietly backstage if they desire.'

George Christie took quickly to the idea of an auditorium in the spirit of an Italian opera house. 'I said to the Hopkinses please go and look at those wonderful Italian theatres in Reggio Emilia, Bologna, Parma and the Fenice. Iain Mackintosh extended this to Bordeaux. Derek Sugden of Arup Acoustics was particularly keen on the recreated Munich Residenztheater, another horseshoe. Another of my favourites is the Margrave's theatre at Bayreuth – the one rejected by Wagner.' Christie feels that the fan 'works wonderfully well at Wagner's Bayreuth theatre, but nowhere else. And despite the fact that my Dad admired Bayreuth as his role model in the 1930s, the original Glyndebourne did not look like Wagner's theatre – except for the bare boards and looking pretty basic. You don't want to copy Bayreuth when your repertory is concentrated on Mozart.'

Mackintosh's second major point was that the new auditorium would have to be significantly larger than the old. 'Good acoustics in an opera house require approximately 7 cubic metres volume per member of the audience – compared to 4 cubic metres for a playhouse and 10 for a concert hall. Yet until recently this simple statistic wasn't known. Look at the Olivier. It's 11 cubic metres per person and people can't hear.'

One of Mackintosh's enthusiasms is for sacred geometry. His early sketches for Glyndebourne were based on the two interlocking circles of auditorium and stage. He explains that 'the two worlds or circles of audience and of actor interpenetrate in the "vesica piscis", the Latin expression for the fish-shaped area where those circles overlap.' He goes further: 'In the "vesica piscis" there is a position of power analogous to that in the crossing in a well-proportioned cathedral. In an opera house this area is inhabited by the conductor, the orchestra and the singers well downstage.'

Michael Hopkins's reaction was benign if quizzical. 'I'll turn Iain's mumbo-jumbo into architecture,' he said. What no one could have anticipated was the positively Euclidean way Hopkins would develop the circular geometry. Whether you are convinced or not by theories of sacred geometry and the 'vesica piscis', there is no doubt that the sophistication of Glyndebourne lies in the remarkable overlay of two geometries – theatrical and architectural.

The brilliance of Michael and Patty Hopkins was to work the geometry right through both the plan and the section of the building. Starting with a single unchanging floor level throughout the stage and backstage areas, they achieved even levels of circulation – so that (with a suitable electronic card) you can circulate throughout the whole building on ground, circle and upper circle levels. Mackintosh says, 'In all classical theatres from the Renaissance onwards, the interior and exterior are doing different things. This is the first time both do the same.'

Once Hopkins began to play with the circular geometry of the auditorium, he took it through to the staircases, foyers and circulation spaces. With this developed the idea of open ambulatories, akin in a way to the open arcades wrapped round Roman theatres. Hopkins explains that when he was in Paris, he 'noticed the arcades around the outside of a theatre at the back of the Palais Royal. If I can run arcades along the

Long section cut through the centre of the auditorium by Theatre Projects Consultants, July 1990. This shows three balconies, shallower than those built, and a flexible proscenium zone with stepped boxes which was superseded by the simpler fixed form finally built

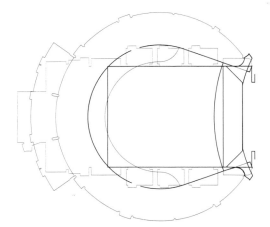

The horseshoe plan of the new Glyndebourne auditorium laid over the shoe-box form of the old. The heavier lines delineate the balcony fronts

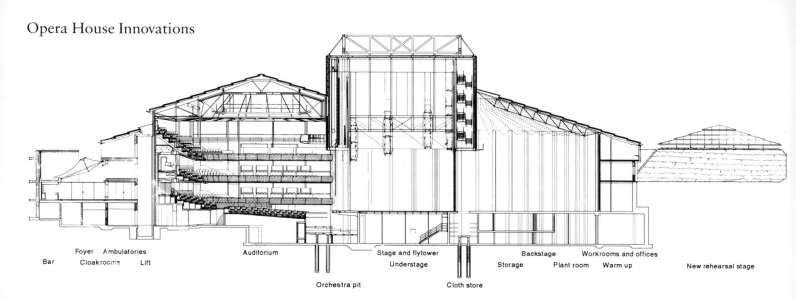

Bar
Foyer Ambulatories
Cloakrooms Lift
Auditorium
Orchestra pit
Stage and flytower
Understage
Cloth store
Backstage
Storage Plant room Warm up
Workrooms and offices
New rehearsal stage

*Michael Hopkins & Partners'
long section through the theatre
illustrating the scale of the spaces
within the new building and its
siting cut into the hillside. The
auditorium seats 400 more
people than the old Opera
House, the proscenium arch is 3
metres wider and the backstage
storage capacity is greatly
increased*

*Plan at foyer level. The
ambulatories, dressing-rooms
and offices are wrapped around
the auditorium, stage and
backstage, giving a human scale
to the external elevations. The
structure of the building relates
to a circular geometry with each
brick pillar set out on the radii of
a circle*

sides at Glyndebourne and around the back, I thought, it will make the exterior more interesting. Gradually I put together the geometry of the auditorium and the ambulatories so you could put a compass at the centre of the auditorium roof and see everything radiating from that point. Then Derek Sugden sent me a postcard of the original Bayreuth, showing marvellous rounded ends, a brick arcade at ground level and what looked like a lead roof.'

The next stage was to extend the circular geometry to the backstage areas. The result is an ellipse – a strongly formed, powerfully contained building rounded at both ends, almost perfectly symmetrical in plan, apart from the turret staircases which are concentrated where they are needed, in the working part of the theatre. A glance at the plan shows that the new Glyndebourne has several skins. The auditorium is circular and double-wrapped for soundproofing purposes. Then comes an inner structural wall – continuous around the stage and backstage – followed by an outer structural wall. This is formed by piers or pillars which are open at the auditorium end and glazed in as offices around the backstage. The remarkable part is the way every structural pier of the inner and outer circle is aligned precisely on regularly-spaced radii. True, the ambulatories, if you look closely, are polygonal rather than continuously curved (as is the auditorium wall); the problem of producing outwards-bulging structural arches would probably have been insuperable apart from being clumsy. But such is the powerful sweep of the ends that this is hardly noticeable to the eye.

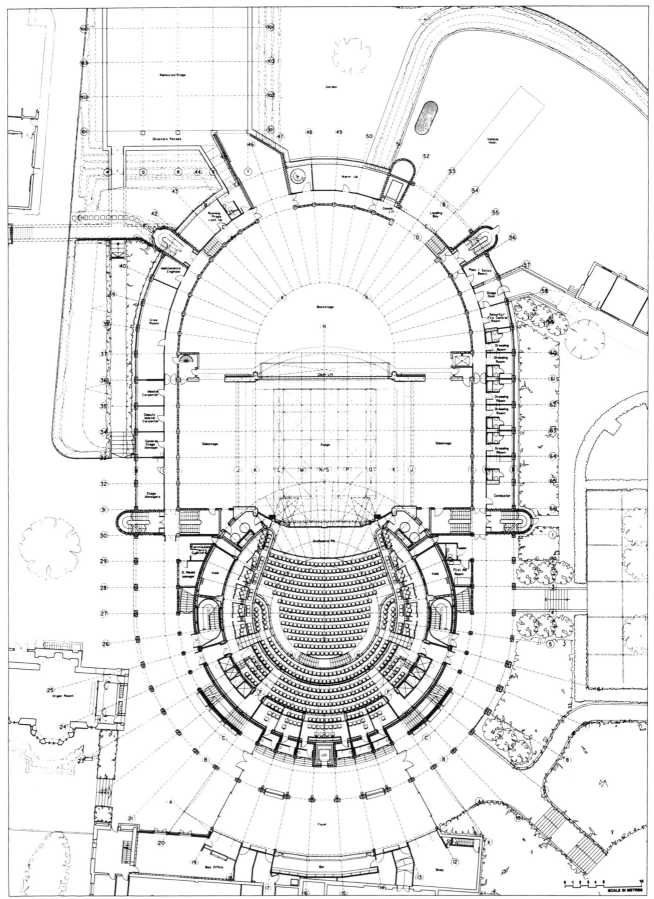

FOYER LEVEL

The Mound Stand at Lords designed by Michael Hopkins & Partners, 1987

Above right and opposite. *The airy canopies of the new foyer at Glyndebourne developed from the Mound Stand at Lords, creating an indoors-outdoors feel*

The round shape was appropriate for a second reason. Glyndebourne never had a front door, and without such a focal point the arcades could simply disappear out of view. A building without a clear beginning or end also melted more easily into the landscape. Michael Hopkins adds, 'The rounded ends made it easier to slide the new building past the Organ Room and fit it in with the dressing-room block.'

One of Hopkins's boldest strokes was to create a tent-roofed foyer that in many ways had the character of a marquee. 'One of my first impressions of the old Glyndebourne was the foyer. It was very much an inside-outside space. A bit draughty at times, but very summery. You came in straight from the garden. There were no doors in between. I wanted to create the same feeling. I'd enjoyed the same feeling in the Mound Stand at Lord's Cricket Ground with its lightweight tented roofs, and these seemed appropriate for Glyndebourne.'

He was very taken, too, by the idea of expressing the inside shapes on the outside: 'Similarly, I wanted the materials on the inside to be familiar from the outside and vice-versa.' In an urban theatre, says Hopkins, there is often no more than a front portico, and this means an interior can be very confusing. 'Spin someone round on stage three times and they won't know which way is front-of-house and which backstage,' he says jokingly.

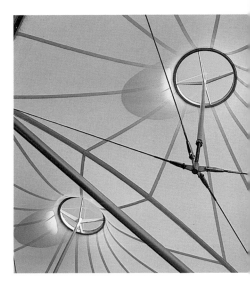

When it came to acoustics, George Christie had stated at the outset that he wanted 'a marriage of flattering resonance with absolute clarity'. But Derek Sugden, best known for his work at Snape Maltings, the home of the Aldeburgh Festival, was well placed to achieve this. A civil and structural engineer by training, he has spent twenty-five years advising on acoustics.

Christie had been concerned that some acousticians would insist on dominating the whole design process and that he would end up with a shoebox auditorium suitable for a concert hall but not an opera house. Sugden, however, was happy to work with the circular geometry. 'An acoustician works through intuition, and through calculation, but we do use precedent a great deal. And here the great precedent was Victor Louis's circular opera house of 1780 in Bordeaux – holding 1,200, though packed a little tighter.'

Circular geometry, he explains, can create focusing problems and the possibility of discrete echoes. 'Old houses are mostly pretty dry – without resonance. Thick carpets, absorbent seating and curtains inhibit echoes and the singers have to work hard. But you can't be as reverberant as a concert hall or you would lose clarity.'

According to Sugden, the quality of an acoustic is very dependent on short delays or time gaps between the direct sound and the first reflections, and also between subsequent reflections. The reverberation time must be long enough in the right frequencies to provide the warmth and richness for music, but not too long or the words can be masked or become unintelligible.

Sugden believed an opera house of 1,150 seats could be evolved with a geometry small enough to ensure a powerful direct sound with short side reflections, yet sufficiently large to ensure a good reverberation time. 'With the right geometry,' he says, 'it is possible to produce a rich sound similar to Bayreuth or Teatro Colón without any sacrifice of intelligibility.'

The keys, in his mind, were to increase volume and to use hard surfaces. 'I started with 8 cubic metres per seat. You have to play safe. As a design develops, you lose volume as the structure and the sight-lines are adjusted and more seats are introduced. Here at least I knew the architect wouldn't be filling the auditorium with carpets and soft furnishings. My

A view taken from the orchestra pit during construction, showing the circular form of the new auditorium ceiling

aim was for a reverberation time of 1.4 seconds. Side reflections were *most* important too – I asked that the balconies should not be more than 17–18 metres apart from side to side.'

Rob Harris, at Arup Acoustics, who acted as acoustic consultant with Derek Sugden, takes up the story: 'The computer programmes we use for testing acoustics in concert halls were not appropriate here because of the circular geometry. Instead we used acoustic scale modelling. The technique is to take a model of the design, made to one-fiftieth scale, and model the people and all the surfaces so they will have equivalent absorption to the real surfaces in the full-scale auditorium. To test the completed auditorium we fire starting pistols; in the model we use a tiny spark to achieve the same effect. We have a tiny microphone and move it around, testing one seat at a time, which enables us to get an impulse response.'

The result of the tests, says Harris, was to show that the original ceiling concept – more in the form of a dome – was not suitable. 'You could see late reflections and focusing problems.' This corresponds with an observation of Sugden's: 'If you look at most of the so-called domes in classical opera houses they're actually flat.'

Harris explains that a curved auditorium can act like a curved mirror. 'Instead of an even distribution of sound, there will be places where the sound is too loud or not loud enough.' In traditional opera houses, 'there was a wealth of rococo ornament. This was very useful as it acted as a sound scattering device.'

Clearly, the Hopkinses are not the kind of architects to introduce ornament into an interior. Harris pays tribute to the way they solved the problem: 'They've taken on the acousticians' bizarre requirements yet it doesn't look as if any special acoustic provisions have been made. It's certainly not like the acoustician's warehouse you sometimes see.' He calls attention to 'the radial ribs of the ceiling and the supports of the circular lighting bridge. The dimensions and size are tailored for an acoustic role. Similarly, the concave wall of the theatre has been faced with convex reflectors to diffuse the sound.'

Glyndebourne regularly has a full house, and it was vital that the acoustics should not be radically different when the seats were empty during rehearsals. Harris tells us that they 'took two dozen seats to a lab in Suffolk, to test the absorption of the seating with and without people. We did this with the local Parish Church Council who got a contribution to church funds in return.'

Another of the acoustician's tasks is to ensure that all outside noise is shut out. Planes coming in to land at Gatwick Airport from the east fly over Glyndebourne before turning. Complete noise insulation was provided by a double skin. 'We used special resilient rubber wall ties between, as in a recording studio,' says Harris. The Glyndebourne auditorium was to be lit by low voltage lights fed by transformers. 'These can buzz, and we had to work carefully to site them where they could not be heard.'

Will George Christie's desire for both pleasing resonance and absolute clarity be met? Rob Harris's answer is that 'Thirty years ago it was thought that you had a choice between reverberation or clarity. And pure clarity means a dead space. Now we know that if you have enough early reflections you can have both.'

Derek Sugden of Arup Acoustics firing a starting pistol to test the acoustics in the new auditorium, December 1993

10

The building in the landscape

THE FLYTOWER had loomed above Glyndebourne since 1938. Even so, the new flytower – its height, bulk, visibility and cladding – posed almost the greatest single compositional problem in the designing of the new opera house. 'I was very anxious that the bulk of the new building should not be hugely greater than before,' says George Christie. 'We lopped off a small amount of height from the flytower at my personal request.'

Concern centred particularly on the famous view of Glyndebourne from the ha-ha at the end of the garden. Michael and Patty Hopkins coped with this partly by turning the theatre around 180 degrees. This meant they could set the new flytower 33.5 metres further back than the old one – more distant from the gardens. As a result, it intrudes less on the view from this point though it is actually higher by 6.7 metres.

George Christie's father had used the slope of the hill beside the house to provide the rake for his auditorium seats. 'It was the easiest building ever to demolish – the bare earth was just under the floorboards,' Christie says with a laugh. As the new auditorium slopes in the opposite direction, no such convenient use could be made of the topography. Instead, the Hopkinses decided to dig deep into the hill. For much of the 1992 season, the main feature of Glyndebourne was a large hole followed by a mass of concrete foundations. Patty Hopkins recalls the Christies becoming 'much happier when they could see the building rising above the ground like a crop.'

Just how deep the Hopkinses cut is evident from the rehearsal stage to the rear curve of the new opera house. Little more than the clerestory windows are visible above the ground.

Originally, the intention was to build the flytower in brick; but Bovis, the main contractors, pointed out that constructing a massive tower in load-bearing brick would greatly lengthen the contract. The Hopkinses personally 'felt it right that the tower should not be brick but an extension of the lead roofs. So lead cladding became very appropriate.' To lessen the sheer solid mass of the top of the flytower, they decided to expose the steel girder frame from which the flytower roof, machinery and walls, were hung.

The entrance to Glyndebourne with the new flytower behind. The flytower is on a direct axis with the archway to the left of the house and the auditorium aligns with the centre of the house

The steel frame of the flytower, December 1992

Backstage during construction, looking straight into the scene dock, February 1993

This is inevitably one of the most controversial aspects of the design because it is so visible – and so frankly industrial in its ethic. Patty Hopkins reflects that they 'could have made the trusses higher and thinner, or lower and fatter. Maybe the members are a bit tough and would have been more joyful if slightly slimmer.' It is possible to imagine a crown of this kind. In the hands of quite a number of high tech architects, a roof such as this would have been an opportunity for a virtuoso display of high tech conjuring – not all of it functional and some definitely for drama.

But that is not the Hopkinses' way. Patty is very definite about this: 'I like its honesty. It shows this is a working place. It proclaims what a tough, difficult, complex business it is to put on operas.'

The Hopkinses softened the bulk of the flytower by adding a powerful projecting bow to the front and back. Needless to say, this is not simply for appearance's sake: the whole space within the flytower had to be kept free for stage equipment and access galleries. The bow at the back contains the escape stairs from the flytower grid and all the smoke extractors. At the front, the curve becomes the curve of the proscenium arch below – and the space between houses theatre rigging, the house curtains and the

supertitle screen. Patty also points out that the bow at the back makes a much easier junction with the radial beams of the backstage area. 'Marrying circular with square would have been much more difficult.'

The radial geometry of the roofs provides one of the keys to blending the opera house with the buildings and landscape around it. Looking at the auditorium roof from the garden and the park beyond, I was reminded of the gradual rounded slope of the apses of churches – both Romanesque and Renaissance. The combination of the conical roof and the matching stretch of shallow roof below even reminded me of the Pazzi Chapel in Florence. But a reader of *The Times* put me right: 'It's a round house,' he declared! And the famous Roundhouse at Camden Town in London is a distinct parallel.

Roofscape from the steps outside the Middle Wallop restaurant. To the left is the backstage roof with a skylight at the top. On the right is the auditorium roof in the shape of a coolie hat. Like many elements, the lead roof panels were prefabricated off-site. Their stepped form ensures better weathering

The newly restored façade of the Organ Room (top) *which almost touches the circle ambulatories. These provide a new elevated panorama of the gardens, parkland and Downs*

The classic view of the south-east front of Glyndebourne from the ha-ha

Drawing by Birkin Haward showing the Opera House nestling within the landscape

The flytower dominates the view from a number of key angles. Architects usually tend to suggest ways of softening, even disguising, flytowers. The Hopkinses have adopted a different tactic: they have given it both presence and power. It looms up behind the entrance front of the house like a Norman keep – it has the proportions of those huge, simple twelfth-century donjons in the Loire valley like Beaugency and Loches. Shorn of castellated detail, these are not picturesque, but tower memorably above the small houses around them.

From the car park – the first view for many visitors – the new opera house stands like a large cruise liner anchored along the quay of a small port. Here the subtlety of Hopkins's geometry is seen in outline. For though the building is ingeniously symmetrical in plan, here its different features stand out forcefully in silhouette. Instead of two semicircular roofs rising to the flytower, the roof of the auditorium is a cone, whereas that over the backstage is a half-circle. The roofs, in coping with this complex geometry, take on an altogether more sweeping form – like a beach shaped by a retreating tide.

Robin Snell, the project architect, explains, 'We were keen that the fly-tower should read in colour and texture as a roof – not a brick wall. That way it would have been more dominant.'

So the flytower is clad in lead panels – which, because they are vertical, are at present a darker tone than the flat lead on the roofs. Roof-leading not only changes with the weather and looks different if wet or dry, but can mellow to a pale silvery white. The Christies particularly liked the light patina of one of the old domes at nearby Glynde Place. Richard Murdoch, the leadwork consultant, says he expects 'the lead cladding round the flytower to weather down gradually to a lighter grey. The north and east sides may take longer, being less exposed to driving rain.'

None the less, it is clear that the flytower will remain, like many flytowers, the most disputed part of the project. 'It's a gasworks,' is one reaction. There is a point here: gasholders are round, like the fronts of the Glyndebourne flytower; they are metal-clad, often with vertical fillets, just like those at Glyndebourne; and they have crisscross bracing akin to the zigzag girders atop the flytower.

My view is that the 'gasholder' metaphor can be much more apparent in photographs than in reality – where the sheer power of the building is what strikes the viewer. And the best gasholders, though long derided, can be splendid structures: I never take the train out of St Pancras Station without marvelling at the majestic trio of gasholders in their black-red-and-white Ivanhoe plumage.

While the flytower remains undisguised, Hopkins has used a variety of subtle devices to reduce the bulk of the rest of the building. The roof sweeps down over the upper storey, finishing in a broad, flat gutter. The top storey is visually treated as part of the roof and is clad in lead. More than this, it actually juts out over the lower two storeys like the covered wall-walk, or *chemin de ronde*, of a French medieval castle.

In every town in England lead mansards have been used as a means of playing down an extra storey, and usually they are ugly. Michael Hopkins reverses the process, making a feature of the lead-clad storey, and it works. This is a technique he evolved earlier on David Mellor's building in Shad Thames near Tower Bridge in London.

Hopkins speaks of mediating between the opera house and its surroundings: 'The stage and the auditorium are two big black boxes at the heart of the building. Around them we wrapped the "people spaces" – the offices, the dressing rooms and the ambulatories.' As a result, the building looks outwards – the whole way round the perimeter – through generous windows or open arcades.

*The Opera House seen from the
end of the pond, November 1993*

No less calculated is the way Hopkins ensured that smaller buildings were interposed between the new opera house and the gardens and approaches. He happily accepted the patchwork walls of the old dressing-room block – right in front of the southern aspect of the new opera house. On the approach from the car park, he reintroduced Mildmay Hall (despite its name an entirely new building).

One of the constraints in designing the new building had been a desire to retain the company tennis court. The sight of white-clad figures leisurely playing tennis used to set the tone of the whole event for many visitors as they arrived. Without the tennis court, the form of the opera house might possibly have been different.

Among the challenges of providing an extra 400 seats was the need for more gardens for picnicking. As Patty Hopkins recalls, 'We had been concerned to keep the tennis court, but then Mary Keen, who was advising on the landscaping, said, "But where are the new enclosed gardens going? We'll have to take the tennis court." She was right. It provided the opportunity to create of series of smaller-scale gardens.'

Mary Keen explains that, 'Although the old gardens, inherited and developed by Mary Christie with help from Christopher Lloyd, were to remain unchanged, three approach gardens from the car park to the new opera house were needed. In these, we wanted to combine reminders of the old place with all the excitement of the new.'

Mary Christie speaks of the Mildmay garden outside the new Mildmay Hall as 'palest pink. I love old-fashioned roses, and they will be

The Figaro Garden being laid out in January 1994, showing the almost completed Mildmay Hall behind

as old-fashioned as you can get without being the sort that flower for just five minutes. I don't at all like bright red or bright yellow.' Next is the Figaro garden, which Mary Keen says 'has something of the last act of *Figaro*. Much of the old Glyndebourne is in the re-sited apple trees, while the recycled paving and bricks have been used in a way that should suggest they were part of the place.' Mary Christie adds, 'There will be blue campanulas as ground cover and roses climbing up the apple trees.'

The surprise will come with the Bourne garden, on the site of the old Dell garden. 'It's a lookout point, with a ramp for wheelchairs and steps with generous landings to picnic on. We thought that as the building is large, here we should have things in proportion. It will be like a jungle with big leaves everywhere – enormous fig trees, acanthus and gunnera.'

Mary Christie also has plans to grow things up the walls of the new opera house. 'Our house, after all, is covered in magnolia, wisteria, clematis and honeysuckle. Michael Hopkins is keen on greenery so there will be planters around the new building.'

All this may take time: George Christie was anxious at the outset not to increase the existing team of gardeners, led by Chris Hughes and helped by Graham Harvey, Giles and Kevin.

Whatever the problems of planting out in the appalling wet weather of early 1994, Mary Christie promises some new delights to greet the audience, beginning with 'big Ali Baba pots along the covered way full of delicious-smelling lilies.'

Above. *Mary Keen, Mary Christie and Chris Hughes, the Head Gardener, discussing plans for the new gardens, October 1991 and Mary Keen's plan showing the new areas of garden. These provide a choice of approaches to the new theatre*

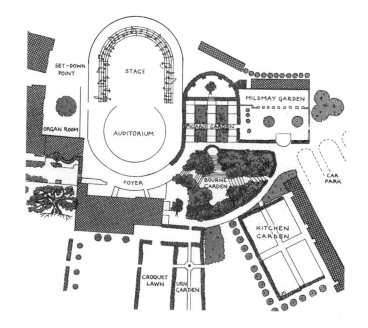

11

Building the new opera house

THE BUILDING of Glyndebourne was a race against time. George Christie had declared that no more than a single season must be lost. Work began in the autumn of 1991 and continued through the 1992 Festival – outside the confines of the old theatre.

Hours had to be strictly controlled. Work stopped every day at 4pm during the Festival Season, and the programme was planned to provide sufficient quiet time for rehearsals. 'The joke was that at least bricks could be laid quietly,' says Robin Snell.

To Bovis fell the task of establishing the tight time-table. Alan Lansdell, the construction manager working for Bovis, explains, 'We programmed it out naturally, and it came out at 22 months. We had to cut it back to 16 and a half months.' Lansdell points out that 'This is a very traditional building. There is no fast-track method of construction. With an office block you might build a steel frame and fill in floors and walls as you go up.' Here it was almost all traditional load-bearing construction – 'proper construction', as Michael Hopkins called it.

Lansdell began by picking out a series of key dates. 'We met every one,' he says with satisfaction. But these were only achieved in two ways – by stockpiling materials and by prefabricating important elements off-site.

At the outset, Robert Chitham of English Heritage had suggested materials similar to those of the old opera house: 'brickwork (perhaps with stone dressings), plain tiled roofs, shingles and joinery of oak.' The Hopkinses studied local buildings in Lewes – brick, tile, stucco, flint – and decided on brick.

Test panels measuring 12 × 6 feet were set up on the old tennis court, and the brick finally chosen, though like a traditional Sussex brick, came from across the Hampshire border at Selborne, best known as the home of the eighteenth-century naturalist Gilbert White. Michael Hopkins points out that they were all 'handmade bricks. We used the old imperials. They're a far better size. The new metric bricks are too big.'

Glyndebourne took over the entire production of the brickworks, and experience during the 1992 season convinced Lansdell that he must build

Detail of one of the ambulatory walls, showing the colour variation in the handmade bricks

View from the tower crane during construction showing the close relationship of the house to the Opera House. The end of the Organ Room, which had disappeared when the first theatre was built, was reconstructed exactly as it looked in 1920

117

up a vast stockpile. 'Bovis would go to Selborne two or three times a week,' says George Christie, 'pay on the nail, and the bricks were stacked up here in the car park.'

Hopkins had set himself a specially difficult task – building well over 400 almost flat arches, the centres rising not more than an inch (25 mm) above the sides. Normally, a virtually flat lintel would have a steel or concrete support. Not with Michael Hopkins. Lansdell explains the first step in making these arches: 'All the bricks were made with clay from the farmyard by the brickworks. The clay was then pushed through a press. All the bricks for one arch would be cut from the single column of clay that came out.'

Snell provides further detail: 'The bricks were cut out with a cheese wire, individually numbered and then fired as a complete arch. The bricks for all the arches were done by two husband-and-wife teams, the wives doing the geometry and the husbands the cutting.'

Normally, the weight of an arch descends into a pillar or pier. Hopkins's arches, being almost flat, had to be wedged between the piers – and the piers are sloped back to give some extra support. (Imagine yourself carrying a loaf of sliced bread between the palms of your hands, concertina fashion: you would press in at the bottom to stop the centre collapsing.)

Stringent tests were carried out to demonstrate that the piers and arches would not crack under loading. Similar tests had to be made with

Bricklayers at work on one of the load-bearing arches for the office accommodation, March 1993

Samples of brickwork were built on the old tennis court for comparison with the mellow brick of the old house, September 1991

Patty Hopkins, Robin Snell and Michael Hopkins assess a sliding window in the mock-up, June 1992

the brickwork for the walls. Patty Hopkins explains the problem: 'We were using solid walls without the normal cavity to break the path of water. These had to be tested for water penetration. They would be watered for so many hours and days – we had to show the construction would stand the weather.'

Next came the laying of the bricks, as described by Lansdell: 'We assembled up to forty bricklayers – that's as many first-class bricklayers as you can find in an area like this.' How did they decide a man was a first-class bricklayer? 'The foreman bricklayer looked at his work for three hours and if he was no good he went.' Lansdell recalls that when they began, there were only two bricklayers who could build an arch, and it would take them five days. 'By the time we finished, there were eight who could do the arches, and it was taking them two to two-and-a-half days an arch.'

Much of the quality of the Glyndebourne brickwork lies in the jointing. Lansdell calls it 'traditional lime putty mortar – the type that was used before the war. The outside edge – exposed to the air – goes hard, but inside it never really sets, so there's always a certain amount of flexibility. With hard modern cement you have to put in expansion joints to stop cracking.'

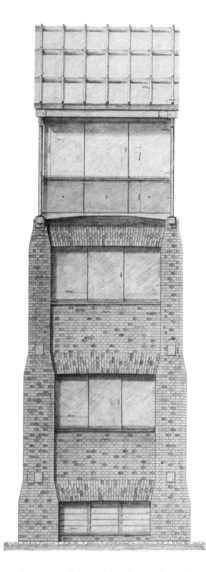

Drawing by Michael Hopkins & Partners showing the load-bearing brick piers and arches in a typical structural bay. The drawing also illustrates the way in which the range of materials used – bricks, lead panels, glass, steel and concrete – were effectively combined

Great care was taken over the colour and texture of the mortar. Snell says that they analyzed 'the sand in the old garden walls and found a similar sea sand – much coarser than the usual builders' sand'. The result is a slightly pinky mortar blending with the brick, and flecked with minute chippings.

The best English brickwork has traditionally been fine-jointed, and Glyndebourne is no exception. According to Snell, joints of 10 mm are common nowadays, but at Glyndebourne they narrowed it down to 8, and 6 in the arches.

While the foundations and substructure were constructed of *in situ* concrete, all the beams and ceiling panels of the ambulatories and auditorium were precast off-site. Patty Hopkins says of the technical problem, 'We could have had wet *in situ* concrete which you plaster over, but *in situ* concrete can be slightly disastrous. With precast concrete you can control the process more rigorously. You can shape the edges, producing the equivalent of mouldings. The problem is you can't make a hole later and plaster and patch it. You have to remember everything – down to the precise position of lights.'

The concrete was precast by two companies – Dynaspan in Ireland, who did much of the external work, and Trent of Nottingham, who cast the panels and beams for the interior. Precision was crucial. Lansdell describes the situation: 'The architect must get the geometry right, then the contractor has to do his own working drawings, checking all the measurements again.' The concrete is formed in wooden moulds or forms. In the auditorium, the panels fit together as closely as the voussoirs of an arch; the greatest challenge lay in the sloping and slightly twisting panels above the entrance to the circle, where the wooden forms were of complex, curving shapes.

The individual ceiling panels weigh up to five or six tons and were most vulnerable when being moved, as the edges could easily be chipped. While being transported, they were stacked on special nylon 'spacers'. Fixing eyes were cast into the top surface so they could be picked up by the crane – in almost the same way, incidentally, as the stones of the Parthenon were manoeuvred into position 2,500 years ago.

Between each adjoining ceiling panel is a gap of just 10 mm. 'Every piece was set out before it was transported to ensure it would fit. There

are only five pieces in the whole auditorium where some tolerance is possible,' says Lansdell with feeling.

All the constructional elements of the auditorium, including the roof, were brought into position by a tower crane standing in the centre of the auditorium and projecting above the roof. Eventually this had to be lifted out by another crane brought in specially. The final challenge came in closing the central hole with a single large concrete 'bung'. This was slowly winched up and fixed to the steels above, like the rest of the ceiling panels.

Snell describes the great care taken with the concrete mix and finish: 'There's a strong sprinkling of mica which sparkles when it catches the light. When the moulds are struck off the concrete, the surface is milky. We wash it with a mild acid which exposes the mica, but leaves the surface smooth and unpitted.'

English Heritage had suggested a roof of tiles or shingles, but in the end another traditional material was chosen – lead. According to Eric Gabriel, the project manager, this is 'probably the largest leadwork contract on any postwar building.'

Watercolour by Robert Bates of the theatre from the car park during construction, April 1993

121

The steel structure of the auditorium roof with the tower crane in the centre used to manoeuvre building materials into place, May 1993

Gary Webb of Broderick's putting the finishing touches to the leadwork contractors' plaque on the roof of the auditorium, September 1993

Opposite. *The steelwork of the flytower was erected at night with the aid of powerful floodlights to accelerate construction while work on other areas continued by day*

The design follows on from the stepped roof of the cutlery factory at Hathersage in Derbyshire which Hopkins designed for David Mellor. The distinctive stepping and ridging are the product of the size of lead sheets used. 'You can't lay lead in continuous sheets,' says Robin Snell. 'The best way of jointing and weatherproofing is to put a step in it.' Once again, the lead roof panels were prefabricated in the factory – the lead laid on top of a plywood roof sandwich. Each panel could come with one ridge preformed in the middle – alternate ridges or rolls would be hand-finished on the roof itself. On this job, there were two main gangs of leadworkers for the roof; Lansdell points out, 'We ensured consistency in laying by using the same people in the factory and on site for each section.'

Building the flytower within the timetable could only be achieved by working on it at night, borrowing the crane that was being used for the auditorium during the day. Six floodlighting towers were brought in and the steel frame was erected after dark. Hopkins explains that 'for speed we built four concrete legs, and then put the steel structure on top and hung everything from it – the lead cladding and the flytower machinery inside.'

John Thornton of Ove Arup, the structural engineers, points out another bonus from this decision: 'Initially we started with a huge banana beam carrying the weight of the flytower over the proscenium arch. The new coat-hanger structure enabled us to shift all the heavy engineering out of the auditorium.'

The joinery of the auditorium was also prefabricated off-site. The idea had always been to have a largely wooden interior in the spirit of the old Glyndebourne. The assumption was that it would be oak; but Hopkins characteristically began to think of something different. 'We didn't want a posh wood. Patty and I went to look at the old theatre at Parma. Originally this was a painted interior, but in its present state, after a fire, the stripped pine is a golden yellow orange. We became very keen on a pine interior. Glyndebourne was never particularly smart. So we used reclaimed pitch pine – a beautifully strong material.'

The wood – vast quantities of it – came from Jeremy Nelson's sawmill on Romney Marsh, and was delivered to Cheesman's the joiners in Aylesford, Kent. Nelson makes clear that it is all 'reclaimed pitch pine, over 100 years old'. The two species of pitch pine, *Pinus palustris* and *Pinus picea*, grew principally along the banks of the Mississippi River. They were brought back as ballast in British ships trading with the Southern States. 'It's a very resinous timber,' according to Colin Cheesman, 'very hard, completely different from Scandinavian pine.'

Above. *Chris Dodds working on one of the curved balcony fronts in Cheesman's joinery workshop. This is seen below* in situ *at the front of the foyer circle*

This timber, Nelson tells us, is salvaged from the docks and the industrial heartlands. 'All through the nineteenth century pitch pine was used for joists, beams and floor boards. From one building under demolition we took 600 beams 32 feet long, all 14×14 or 15×15 inches, as well as a 140,000-foot run of floor boards. Whisky bonds are another good source of pitch pine. The distillers were connoisseurs of the wood, and had a lot of purchasing power. They could compete with the Navy.'

As it was old timber, a metal detector had to be used to find nails and bolts buried in it. After being cut to precise measurements, it was delivered to Cheesman's, who had hired a special warehouse to set it out. The

The upper ambulatory provides a spectacular view of the landscape. The steel trusses are framed in elegant pencil-shaped pitch-pine beams

One of the pair of matching flights of steps leading up to the back of the stalls. The majority of the woodwork in the auditorium is reclaimed North American pitch-pine which is mellow in colour and richly patterned

old wood was very dark and dirty, but straightforward planing revealed a mature colour you would never get with new wood.

The most testing task was the shaping of the balcony fronts. These were not only curved and occasionally serpentine, but bombé. The complex setting-out in the workshop was done by Chris Dodds, whom Cheesman describes as 'the one with the brains to do the drawings and the maths'.

Each panel was made of six boards, and 'on some balustrades twenty-odd jigs were needed to create the shape', says Cheesman. The need for precision was unusually great; Lansdell explains that you can normally rely 'to some extent on make-up pieces and cover moulds to hide blemishes, but here you have none'.

Another problem lay in filling all the nail and bolt holes. As Cheesman explains it, 'We fill these with little boat-shaped pieces – literally thousands of them. We make them boat-shaped because they're less noticeable than round or square pieces and it's easier to match the grain.'

The beauty of the finished woodwork is that it is both mellow and extraordinarily smooth. It is the resin in the wood, says Cheesman, that 'gives it a waxy feeling – we've just given it a clear coat of beeswax which should be repeated every two years.' He also anticipates little problem from heating, as Glyndebourne is principally a summer opera house. 'Nor should there be a problem with humidity. The resin stops it getting in. A large audience, of course, produces humidity, but the air conditioning will carry that away.'

The highly resinous wood presented more of a problem with the wall panels when they were transported to Nottingham to be fire-proofed. Because of the resin, it was no easy task to impregnate them.

Jeremy Nelson also made the flitch beams – 230 in all – which support the roof of the upper ambulatory. These narrow elegantly to pencil points at the end, and consist of a steel plate sandwiched between two pitch pine boards. Nelson describes the process: 'We had to select these carefully, so that none had more than six knots or four bolt holes. That's to ensure the strength of the wood.' As you would expect with Michael and Patty Hopkins, the timber is not simply for appearance's sake. As Nelson puts it, 'It's not only structural. The wood would protect the metal from buckling in a fire.'

Glyndebourne was fortunate to be building in a recession – achieving a quality of craftsmanship which might not have been possible at other times within a strict budget. George Christie recognizes that they 'picked up the cream of the trades'.

If Alan Lansdell was responsible for bringing in the building on time, it was Eric Gabriel's task to complete it within budget. Gabriel acted as the client's project manager – previously he had worked on the National Gallery extension in London and came with the recommendation of Lord Rothschild. 'I provide the single point link between the contractor and the Glyndebourne staff', Gabriel says. 'I authorize all expenditure and payments. The cost control system involved authorization of all changes and additional costs. We did this at weekly meetings held first in London – where most of the design was done – and then on site.'

Gabriel operates what he calls the DTR system. 'It stands for design team recommendation. Any change has to be identified by those making it. It's not a paperwork system. It's all decided face to face. Everyone must notify Bovis of the changes. That means Bovis will pick them up, if people don't realize they've made a change.'

He has a maxim: cost and time cannot be separated. 'The paradox was that to succeed on budget we had to keep to time. At times we had to make extraordinary efforts. Alan Lansdell would come to me and say, there's a problem. We could miss a key date. I would say we have to work round the clock for a few days or order a material at a premium.'

The one thing that kills projects is changes, according to Gabriel: 'All changes are bad for the client and the project. But inevitably you have to develop the design.' He identifies three categories of change. 'If something is essential I authorize it. If it's simply nice to have I say no. But there's an intermediate category. Things you ought to have but which could delay the project. We had a lot of those in the last three months of the contract. I'd say: defer them till we finish. Don't stop Bovis. Most of them we were able to do in January.'

George Christie is warm in his praise of his team. 'Eric Gabriel was gold dust for us. Bovis I can't fault. Alan Lansdell is a gritty individual with a huge heartbeat, a man of incredible confidence, dedication and passion.'

The curving balcony front on circle level, showing the 'twinkle' lights

12

The auditorium

GEORGE CHRISTIE gave three reasons for choosing a horseshoe-shaped auditorium: intimacy, acoustics, and quite simply the beauty of the shape. He has triumphed. Here is grand opera in a warm, engaging setting, and an interior which is both modern and born of tradition. More than this, it has the sense of being one thing, an absolute conceptual unity, all of a piece in the way that an eighteenth-century wooden ship was.

Visually, its beauty has four main aspects: it is all in the round; it is predominantly of wood; the colour scheme is stunning; and the lighting is infinitely subtle.

Circular plans have fascinated architects throughout the centuries, but rarely has an architect been able to take the discipline of circular geometry and apply it systematically to every aspect of design and fitting-out. Seating, galleries, gangways, ceiling and proscenium arch all take their form from a series of concentric and overlapping circles and their radii. Colin Cheesman, who did the woodwork, points out that the floor is not flat but gently 'dished'. Even the floor boards of the gangways around the stalls fan out in a serpentine curve, first concave then convex. The seats of the stalls are not in straight lines, but a series of gentle arcs. Look at the bombé balcony fronts: the swell varies not only from level to level but from one length to another. Look at the backs of the boxes at the sides: these are convex, for acoustic reasons, to provide reflections. So are the acoustic panels around the walls in the upper circle; and even the panels in the vertical sides of the recessed ceiling are convex.

The whole wall containing the proscenium arch surges out in a forceful curve, picked up by the arc of the advance lighting bridge above. Even the sides of the bridge are bowed almost like the walls of a tyre, increasing the sense of tension.

A further subtlety lies in the lyre-shaped seating in the foyer circle, raised above the stalls but still below the level of the stalls circle behind. This is one of Iain Mackintosh's favourite features. 'I've always been very fond of this shape – you found it in Wyatt's Drury Lane and still find it in the Bayerisches Staatsoper in Munich. It comes in Saunders's treatise of 1790 on theatres. The way it returns here into the gallery front comes from Munich.'

Looking into the stalls from the red side. The lamps on the right-hand side are for the production and lighting desk which is situated in the stalls during rehearsals, allowing both ready access to the stage and a view of the opera as the audience will see it

Will Bonner drilling out the holes for the individual seat pedestals, October 1993. A continuous supply of fresh air enters the auditorium gently and noiselessly through the perforations in the pedestals

The second beauty of the interior is that it is so largely in wood and particularly in salvaged pitch pine. What is so remarkable is the sheer consistency, not only of major elements like the balcony fronts, but the numerous partitions behind and between the seats and boxes, and the panelling behind.

The third beauty lies in the colour scheme. Opera houses are generally associated with white and gold, velvet and plush. The old Glyndebourne was, of course, very different, but the crucial decision in the new auditorium was to evoke its character and to eliminate colour. Instead, there is only the lustre of the woodwork, the subdued neutral tone of the concrete, and the bold, starling black of the proscenium arch and the house curtain. Just as a dinner jacket might be midnight blue, the curtain is not true black, but a very dark grey. It is matched by the charcoal grey upholstery of the seats.

Patty Hopkins describes the dilemmas that preceded the choice. 'We had long discussions on the colour of the seats and the house curtain. We were always rather keen on grey. We started with a grey flannelly curtain which the Christies thought – rightly – would look too conference-y. We thought of green and claret red, but the production people were very keen for the curtains to be a non-colour. The old house curtain had been green and many designers would not use it because it clashed with their sets.

'In desperation I went to John Lewis on the way to a 10 o'clock meeting and bought a rather beautiful dark grey velvet skirt fabric. The Christies fell in love with it at once and we copied the colour for both seats and house tabs.'

After much thought, they decided that no more colour was needed. 'Green or red would have been too much with the timber and brick.' But Patty accepts the description 'smart' with just a little reluctance: 'It's certainly not Ritzy!' she says.

The black is picked up in striking ways elsewhere in the auditorium – in the advance lighting bridge, and in the proscenium which is faced in the same lead panels as the flytower, though here it will not oxidize and fade with exposure to the elements.

Patty Hopkins explains that all the theatrical advisers said the proscenium must be 'dark, not reflective. An ornate gilt proscenium can create problems by reflecting lights. So the proscenium consists of no

The sweep of the upper circle showing the high-backed seats that obviate the need for a handrail

more than matt lead panels and a simple steel frame to the opening, painted a very dark grey.'

For some productions and producers the black proscenium may be too strong and too dark. But Robin Snell points out that 'The arch has been designed so it can be dressed – completely changed in character, if desired.'

The fourth quality of the auditorium is the lighting, which was so important to George Christie from the beginning. The Hopkinses retained George Sexton, veteran of many acclaimed museum and gallery lighting schemes, to advise them. The beauty of the scheme lies in the sheer number and softness of the lights – creating the atmosphere of candlelight. The small uplighters built into the back of the gallery ceiling panels flare like candle flames. The numerous spots built into the ceilings add to the myriad pinpricks of light seen across the auditorium. The most hotly debated were the lights on the fronts of the balconies. Dubbed 'George's Blackpool twinklies' by their critics, they are the key to the luminosity of the whole auditorium. They add the crucial sparkle to the surfaces that are closest to the eye.

The view from the upper circle. The new theatre offers no fewer than eight front rows on the centre line, and the most distant seat is 3 metres closer to the stage than in the old auditorium

One of the new Glyndebourne signs. The tradition of the old theatre is maintained with red for the prompt side and blue for the o.p. side

The boxes on circle level (left) *and the raised lyre-shape circle at the back of the stalls which is important for acoustic as well as aesthetic reasons*

equivalent of one person standing above another – in case, for example, the stage is raked. Supertitles have to be visible, as well as the head of the proscenium arch from under the balconies. Ideally, as many people as possible should see the conductor's head.'

Horseshoe forms – or indeed any configuration with balconies and boxes – are sometimes criticized as being undemocratic. Anthony Whitworth-Jones, Glyndebourne's General Director, fiercely rejects this. 'Our intention was positively to take advantage of different levels and create a price structure that would enable a wider range of people to come to Glyndebourne.'

One of Theatre Projects' key contributions was to provide, at the outset, an exact seating plan for such a price structure. In 1994 there will be standing room at £10, contrasting with a maximum price of £100. For £15 there are seats in the slips, surprisingly close to the stage in the upper circle, with a clear, though inevitably partial, view.

The continuous open slope of a fan may place everyone in the same space, but Mackintosh turns the point around. 'I like fragmenting the audience into groups, so you don't feel as if you're in a big cinema. You can't get directly from the stalls to the raised lyre shape behind. Complexities like this add interest and make the place more special.'

The rake of the stalls is a crucial calculation. Make it too steep and the whole auditorium becomes too high. Make it too shallow and the

view may be blocked by heads in front. For this, Anne Minors has a simple formula, not unlike John Christie's for the first theatre. 'You should see between the heads in the row in front of you and over the heads of those beyond.'

A distinctive feature of the upper circle is the high-backed seats. These have a double function – partly acoustic, but also obviating the need for a handrail. They also neatly screen the knees of anyone in the row above from view.

Seats in 'the gods' can feel precipitous, particularly if you have a straight view down a gangway to the stage. Mackintosh says that this has been avoided 'by ensuring you can approach the higher seats only from

The singers' view of the auditorium from the stage

137

the sides. This is important, as these seats will be used by older people as well as the young.'

Finding your way easily to your seat undoubtedly helps to put people at ease. Robin Snell reminds us that 'Glyndebourne has always had a red side and a blue side, and we've continued the system. There's one door on each side at each level which splits, going one way to the boxes, the other to the seats.'

For sheer drama and surprise, the best first view of the auditorium is to be had on entering the stalls. As at Covent Garden, you can approach up a flight of steps on the central axis, but here the flight divides. Mackintosh points out that 'This is in fact what Barry designed for the Royal Opera House, though the fools changed it a few years later.' Equally good are the two side entrances to the stalls – the drama being increased by the surprise on emerging from a low-ceilinged corridor into the full height of the auditorium.

The old Glyndebourne, says Michael Hopkins, was a place where you could easily fall asleep. No longer. Glyndebourne has a huge but silent system of air conditioning. John Berry of Arup, the engineers, explains how this was achieved. 'Derek Sugden had set very low noise levels; almost the threshold of hearing – the level at which you can hear a mouse wag its tail.' The solution was to place all the machinery outside the acoustic envelope. 'The pumps and chillers were placed in a totally separate building, a rebuilt potting shed, and linked by an underground tunnel. The air is moved in very large ducts. We're talking of the dimensions of railway carriages. They measure 3 metres by 2½.'

The trick is to bring the fresh cool air in under every seat – through perforations in the pedestal. No one will feel a draught – the air is moving at a rate of 1 metre every 10 seconds. Heat naturally rises, and if the air conditioning outlets were set in the ceiling or upper walls, air would have to be blown at 13–14 °C rather than 18–19 °C. So Glyndebourne saves on energy bills.

The same system ventilates the orchestra pit, where cool air wafts gently in through a large grille on the back wall. Berry says that orchestras often complain about conditions, 'and I have a lot of sympathy with them'.

One serious problem in some opera houses is that dust is lifted from the stage as the safety curtain rises. 'Opera singers make this complaint about well-known houses. We built a 1:25 scale perspex model and tested it at Cambridge in the Department of Applied Mathematics and Theoretical Physics – Stephen Hawkin's department. This showed that a 3° difference on either side of the curtain could cause an air movement of 60 cubic metres a second on the stage. The solution is a management one – to ensure the temperature is reasonably equal on both sides of the curtain before it rises – generally the stage is warmer and the cold air wafts in.'

Where would Michael Hopkins choose to sit in his new auditorium? 'I like the side where you're very aware of the audience opposite. I'd go right round on the corner of the upper circle – as an architect – to experience the performance and the opera house at the same time. You may not get the best sight-lines but you hear very well and you're very close to the stage. It's a sensation I noticed on the Mound Stand, which is on a pronounced curve – there's an added excitement in seeing the audience enjoying the spectacle as much as yourself – and it's heightened at Glyndebourne because the curve is so much sharper.'

Intimacy is important not only to the audience but also to the singers, and their judgment on the auditorium is as important as anyone's. Hopkins is well aware of this. 'We have taken the geometry of the horseshoe right up to the proscenium. From the stage you feel you can stretch out and touch it.'

One of the foyer circle boxes

13

On stage and backstage

FOR GLYNDEBOURNE, the new opera house represents a change from often makeshift arrangements that have evolved from year to year to a custom-built theatre of a most sophisticated kind.

The new technological systems were designed by Alan Russell of Theatre Projects – stage lighting, stage rigging and machinery and sound. 'The aim,' he says, 'was to produce equipment that was both comprehensive and easy to use.'

The first gain is space. The demands at Glyndebourne may not be so great as a major city opera house staging dozens of productions a year. But Glyndebourne has a very intensive season of more than seventy performances, with operas changing nightly. In addition, the touring company gives at least ten performances on its home ground after the main season.

Glyndebourne prides itself on the quality and intensity of its rehearsals. Anthony Whitworth-Jones declares that 'The essential advantage for artists of coming to Glyndebourne – and of course this does not change – is the atmosphere of the place, which is conducive to very intensive and concentrated rehearsals. During the season the rehearsal stage is used every day. Our normal practice is to rehearse the next opera to open on the actual stage in the morning. At the end of the morning, we wheel the whole set into the rehearsal stage, where rehearsals can continue, and set up that evening's opera on stage. At the end of the performance – or early the next morning – that set is wheeled back off the stage, making way for the next morning's rehearsal.'

This can mean that Glyndebourne is dealing with up to five sets at the same time.

The old theatre suffered from the limitation of having only one side stage – on the o.p. side. Tom Redman, the technical director, explains: 'Any production where we were bringing on a large truck – that's a section of scenery on wheels – for example, a ship – we had to take it out again on the same side. Now a whole set for an individual act can be brought in from both sides.'

The construction of the backstage area is naturally plain, but still of interest. The walls are of load-bearing brick – thinner at the top where the

View taken on the day of the press conference on 31 January 1994 to announce the completion of the new theatre. Taken from one of the backstage bridges, it looks from the scenery storage area, across the stage and into the auditorium. Such a vista is only possible when the two safety curtains at the front and back of the stage are raised

The top-lit backstage scenery store with the safety curtain down allowing work to continue during rehearsals

Opposite above. The rehearsal stage which enables one opera to be rehearsed on the main stage and another on the rehearsal stage at the same time. The Douglas fir plywood panels on the walls perform an acoustic function

load is less. These are common bricks – made with the same clay but smoother than the facing bricks which are dipped in sand before they are put in the kiln to give them texture.

The eye is caught by the intense black of the curved drum containing the backstage fire curtain. This is a continuation of the bow of the fly-tower above, which can be seen through the roof light. According to Robin Snell, 'in theatres they generally paint the inside of the flytower black. We've saved them the trouble by adding the black pigment to the concrete.'

The ropes and pulleys operating the flying scenery and cloths block access to the side stage if they descend to the ground. The new Glyndebourne has avoided this, thanks to a double-purchase flying

system. The counterweights, instead of descending to the ground, are hitched up in a double loop leaving a huge clearance height from the stage. Simon Stone, the head flyman, takes particular pride in the new system – 'the first to be operated entirely by new lightweight hardened nylon pulleys'.

At the back of the main stage is another vertically rising steel curtain, almost the same size as the proscenium arch. This is both a fire barrier and an acoustic barrier. On each side, similar narrower steel doors open onto the side stages. These slide sideways as they do not have the height of the flytower to rise into. As a result, the whole backstage area, a generous half-circle 38 metres across, can be used as a working area while rehearsals continue on the other side of the curtain.

On the curving perimeter wall of the backstage are two large doors. One is the dock door. There is a loading bay outside with a vehicle lift on which lorries can be lowered, and scenery and props wheeled off the lorry at tailboard level.

The second door opens into the rehearsal stage, and is the same height so scenery and props can be wheeled or carried through. All through the backstage area there is a clear working height of 9.25 metres allowing sets to be moved freely.

Across the door to the rehearsal stage are two miniature bascule bridges (twin drawbridges like those of Tower Bridge), one above the other, which link with the corridors around the building. When the bridges rise, the handrails first fold down so they fit tight against the wall, preventing any access through the door.

The zigzag metal structure supporting the backstage roof is a development of the roof Hopkins designed for David Mellor's cutlery factory (it also has a happy echo of the roofs at Lewes Station). Robin Snell says that, at the Mellor factory, 'we used tubular steel trusses and ties, which all had to be welded. Here we're using steel angles and ties which have simple bolt fixings – more the way the Victorians did it.'

The bascule bridges which rise in the centre, allowing large scenery to be moved from backstage into the rehearsal stage

The grid 65 feet above the stage which houses all the machinery necessary to raise and lower the safety curtains, house curtain, lighting bridges and backcloths

Looking across the stage and back to the scene dock when the building had just been completed. The three lighting bridges above the stage are clearly visible. Within the flytower there is space for up to 75 backcloths to be flown

One of the chorus dressing-rooms

Another clever device, the first of its kind in Britain, is the cloth store immediately behind the backstage curtain. This is a narrow, long lift in the floor which descends below-stage. It stops at four levels, on each side of which are slotted 16-metre-long trolleys – in profile like the trucks used in coal mines. Alan Russell, who devised it, explains: 'Each one is deep and long enough to store all the cloths from a particular production. The containers are brought up to stage level and the cloths can be detached from the scenery bar housed in the flytower, and rolled up by the stage hands. Below stage they are stored in the containers out of the way in dry, dust-free conditions.'

As well as the scenery, the flytower contains three suspended lighting bridges for front, centre and backstage lights. Each one has two decks; these can be used by actors and singers who are making an entrance from above, whether Monteverdi deities, or Puck flying in to land on a tree.

In the old theatre, as Keith Benson explains, 'there were 200 lights to be moved or adjusted every day. In the new theatre there are 320; of these 235 can still be moved at the director's wish, but the 85 permanently focused lamps can be colour-changed at the touch of a button.'

The main advance in lighting is the much greater clarity. 'We have gone for condenser optics,' says Benson, which provides superb optical output. We're the first in this country to have these lights in such numbers.'

The most careful thought was naturally given to the orchestra pit. George Christie says that the aim was 'to have an orchestra pit made flexible by a rising floor. That way you can achieve the right balance between the singers and the orchestra. For example, if we are doing a production using period instruments, we raise the floor, otherwise they would have to play at full volume, which is not good for the instruments or the sound.'

Derek Sugden, who worked out the precise form, explains that 'You have to be able to adjust from one opera to another. Strauss's *Elektra* has an orchestra of 104. If space for all these were in front of the proscenium, it would kill the architecture, as well as the sound balance. Equally, Berg's *Lulu*, though it has a small orchestra, has so much percussion it would upset the balance, especially for young singers. So I'm an exponent of the semi-covered orchestra pit – with a larger orchestra partly underneath.'

With this goes a state-of-the-art sound system, the latest advance on the rolling boulders which provided the thunder at Drottningholm. Benson elaborates: 'We have a 32-speaker ambionic system. You can create a rifle shot ricocheting right round the auditorium, and there are wonderful bass speakers for thunder effects.'

The two major parts of the operation still housed outside the new building are the production departments, props and wardrobe; but the wardrobe, too, has a new building – a large and striking barnlike structure designed by the Miller Bourne Partnership. The new dyeing room is the best facility in the country, according to the wardrobe manager Tony Ledell, and they now have a millinery department for the first time.

The lighting box at the back of the circle from where the lights are controlled throughout the performances

14

Conclusion

WHEN I first saw the new Glyndebourne I was astounded by its powerful presence. George Christie had asked for an 'architectural statement' at the outset, and Michael and Patty Hopkins have provided it. Looking at black-and-white photographs beforehand, I had certain misgivings. The girder-topped flytower looked positively industrial, the arcades – or ambulatories – a little dour. But in reality it does not strike me this way. In a rush of enthusiasm I wrote, 'Glyndebourne is not just a triumph but a great masterpiece.' Having had the opportunity to study it in detail, my view remains unchanged.

The new Glyndebourne is outstanding, first because the whole building is thought through with the utmost rigour. For all the complex activities it houses, the Hopkinses have produced a design of great simplicity and consistency.

Michael and Patty Hopkins have abided by the modernist beliefs of structural honesty and truth to materials, yet produced a building that is supremely well made and well finished. Patty Hopkins puts it simply: 'As the design progressed, we became very keen on seeing what the building would be made of.'

When George Christie first announced his thoughts of rebuilding the auditorium, he said cautiously that it could not conceivably materialize in less than half-a-dozen years, if ever. It is a tribute to his drive and infectious enthusiasm that the whole project – fund-raising, design, construction and fitting-out – has been completed, as he proudly puts it, 'on time and on budget', just seven years later.

Throughout the project, Christie has fulfilled the classic role of patron. In Patty Hopkins's view, 'George has very good instincts about even quite complex and technical matters. He could disagree and be right.' Following the resignation of Peter Hall, Glyndebourne had no artistic director when some of the designs were being drawn up. The client-architect relationship became crucial. The result is an unusually clearly defined building in shape, silhouette and internal layout. In certain ways, this may limit flexibility, but flexibility can be at the expense of strength of character.

Both the quality and the limitations of the design will be a subject of excited discussion throughout the new theatre's life – and indeed they

Entering one of the theatre boxes at circle level. Scenery for Stravinsky's The Rake's Progess, *designed by David Hockney, is set up on stage*

149

were throughout the design process. Architects, acousticians and theatrical advisers all have different priorities and even different goals. A great design is the result of constant creative discussion, not to say sparring, among them.

One debate at Glyndebourne concerned the proscenium arch – both its size and its character. John Bury had originally proposed a width of 10.5 metres, compared with the 8.8 metres of the old house, and had provided a fan-shaped auditorium plan that would have given 1,200 seats with good sight-lines – all in all, meeting George Christie's basic requirements. The change to a horseshoe-shaped auditorium led to the wider proscenium arch sought by the technical director, Tom Redman, which now measures 11.6 metres. In the process, the auditorium has become bigger. Intimate may no longer be the appropriate word. It is breathtaking. It is also warm, welcoming and friendly. The generous proportions give the interior nobility without losing closeness to the stage.

As for the character of the proscenium arch, there was even a debate as to whether there should be one at all. Iain Mackintosh, in his penetrating book *Architecture Actor and Stage*, argues that 'It is only in the mid-19th century, as the Romantic movement flowered, that a picture frame was interposed between auditorium and stage. Then the forestage, which, as in the Georgian playhouse, had projected into the auditorium, was cut back until, by the beginning of the 20th century, its existence, even in theatres as late as E. M. Barry's Royal Opera House Covent Garden, had been forgotten.'

John Bury explains further: 'We were very keen to have flexibility in the front area. We designers spend our time building platforms out over the orchestra pit and taking the front round into the auditorium.'

The early sketches of the auditorium produced at Theatre Projects (by an outstanding young draughtsman, Gary Overton) show the box looking directly onto the stage with no proscenium arch. John Bury continues, 'We also spend our time making life hell for the orchestra by changing the stage. Then the management puts its foot down and says, no more expense of this kind.'

Both Bury and Mackintosh favoured the idea of stepped boxes close to the stage – an attractive feature of many theatres. But in the end, it was the Hopkinses' rigorous search for logic and clarity that led to the even

Looking out from under the foyer canopy, which is on a direct axis with the terrace in front of the house and Organ Room

Michael Hopkins in conversation with the project architect, Robin Snell, in the foyer on the day of the acoustic test, 28 March 1994

sweep of the balcony fronts, which to my mind is one of the great beauties of the interior.

Yet out of the crucible of the design process have come ideas for other forms of opera house that could be built in the future. There is Bury's thought of a true German court theatre with a horseshoe surrounded not by open balconies but by boxes 'each totally divided'. Derek Sugden has another thought for 'an opera house of shoebox form, or a courtyard opera as I prefer to call it – something on the lines of the Salle Garnier at Monte Carlo, or Drottningholm.'

Undoubtedly Glyndebourne was extraordinarily fortunate in its timing. The major part of the fund-raising was accomplished in what now seem the boom times of the late 1980s. Construction took place at the depth of the recession when prices had never been more competitive. Patty Hopkins says, 'It was a tight budget. There is a lot of construction there for the price. Remember, the building contract itself was for £23 million, not the £33 million for the whole project.'

What is left to do? One key element of the Hopkinses' proposals remains for the future. 'Our original intention was that the restaurants should be rebuilt in the old dressing-room block between the new opera house and the gardens. There were to be two ways through to the bar – at first floor and garden level. It was decided – probably rightly – that this would involve too much building, so the restaurants remained in the Wallops. I hope the plan can be carried out in the future, for there is a simple clarity in walking out of the auditorium in one direction, first to dinner and then into the garden.'

Costume designs by John Gunter for Susanna and Figaro in the 1989 production of Le nozze di Figaro, *revived for the opening night of the new Opera House. The first theatre also opened with this opera in 1934*

A second possibility concerns Glyndebourne's own collections. There is now a well-run archive, but in addition there is a remarkable legacy of costumes and props, many by very talented designers, which are only occasionally seen. The new theatre, precisely because it is so architectural, even Roman in character, offers little space for picture-hanging or display cases. Here, surely, is a project for some future benefactor.

This book is written before the first performance, and indeed before the first big acoustic test on 28 March. Derek Sugden says, 'I never give a

152

verdict on acoustics until I have had the reaction of the singers and the conductor.' In this sense, any verdict at this moment on the new Glyndebourne is premature. But this is a subject on which George Christie has strong, clear views. 'The important thing is to leave the acoustic test till it is too late to make any major changes. If time is available, you can be sure people will want to adjust things. It will cost a lot of money and make things worse than before.'

With relish George Christie tells the story of a new opera house which carried out an acoustic test. 'They put in a dummy audience of sacks filled with sawdust, all with painted faces. I don't know why they didn't just invite people in off the street. After the test, they changed it and they still got it wrong.'

Christie has triumphed because he has been able at every stage to draw the very best from everyone involved in the project. In choosing a building that is so precise and definite and strong a statement, he may simply have been prescient. It may just be rather difficult to alter the building significantly in the future anyway – for without question it is destined to become one of the prime Grade I listed buildings from the 1990s.

Preliminary design by Richard Hudson for Tatyana in Act III Scene 1 of Tchaikovsky's Eugene Onegin, *a ball in Prince Gremin's house. One of two new productions in the opening season of the Opera House*

Peter Grimes *by Benjamin Britten, 1992. Stephan Drakulich (Peter Grimes) and Alan Opie (Balstrode) sing, 'O tide that waits for no man, spare our coasts'. This opera is also scheduled for performances during the opening season of the new house*

153

Notes to the text

1. Manor to mansion

1 *The Works of William Hay*, vol.2, 1794
William Hay lived at Glyndebourne from 1695 to 1755.

2 The late Geoffrey Gilbertson, Stage Manager and House Manager, 1957-91, conversation with Rosy Runciman, 15 February 1991

3 *Victoria County History of Sussex*, vol.1, p.237

4 *Parochial History of Glynde* by the Rev W. de St Croix. Sussex Archaeological Collections, vol. XX, 1868. Subsequently repeated in other volumes, e.g. *Compendious History of Sussex* by M.A. Lower, vol.1, 1870

5 Public Record Office, reference C109, boxes 15-17

6 Ringmer History Newsletter, no. 50, January 1988

7 *The Works of William Hay*, *op. cit.*, vol.1

8 Public Record Office, C109, 17(I)

9 *The Works of William Hay*, *op. cit.*, vol.1

10 *Ewan Christian, A Memoir* by J. Standen Atkins, RIBA Journal XVIII, 1911

11 *Christie of Glyndebourne* Being recollections of her family narrated by Charlotte Brookes after her 80th year, 1919

12 *A Survey of Glyndebourne* by David and Barbara Martin, ROHAS Report no. 1094, 1990

13 *The Victorian Country House* by Mark Girouard, Oxford, 1971

2. The beginnings of a musical tradition

1 John Christie to Walter Edwards during his interview for the position of company accountant, May 1920. Edwards became one of John Christie's most trusted advisers and worked for Christie until he retired in 1953.

2 John Christie, letter to Lady Rosamond Christie, 9 January 1917

3 John Christie, letter to Lady Rosamond Christie, 31 December 1918

4 John Christie, letter to Lady Rosamond Christie, 16 April 1919

5 John Christie, letter to Lady Rosamond Christie, 4 August 1919

6 John Christie, letter to Lady Rosamond Christie, 4 April 1923

7 John Christie, letter to Lady Rosamond Christie, 22 December 1918

8 John Christie, letter to Lady Rosamond Christie, 21 February 1919

9 John Christie, letter to Lady Rosamond Christie, 26 November 1919

10 Jason Warre, conversation with Rosy Runciman, 1992

11 *Wiltshire* by Nikolaus Pevsner. Revised by Bridget Cherry. The Buildings of England (2nd ed.), Harmondsworth, 1975

12 John Christie, letter to Lady Rosamond Christie, 30 March 1919

3. 'We are the Music Makers . . .'

1 *We are the Music Makers* by A.W.E. O'Shaughnessy, 1874

2 John Christie, letter to Lady Rosamond Christie, 11 November 1931

3 John Christie, letter to Lady Rosamond Christie, 16 March 1932

4 Audrey Christie, letter to John Christie, 28 September 1932

5 John Christie, letter to Audrey Christie, September 1932

6 John Christie, letter to Audrey Christie, 22 September 1932

7 John Christie, letter to Audrey Christie, 29 September 1932

8 John Christie, letter to Lady Rosamond Christie, 25 May 1933

9 'I thought it was a crazy idea': Carl Ebert, interview for the BBC, July 1957

10 John Christie, letter to Lady Rosamond Christie, 8 April 1934

11 Professor F.H. Shera, *Sheffield Fete*, 1 May 1934

4. Building on success

1 John Christie, interview for the BBC, 1 June 1955

2 *Sussex* by Ian Nairn and Nikolaus Pevsner. The Buildings of England, Harmondsworth, 1965

3 John Christie, letter to C.L. Nelson, 30 June 1936

4 John Christie, letter to Edmund Tracey, music critic of *The Observer*, 18 June 1959

5 Reginald Tribe, cassette tape sent to Rosy Runciman, February 1993

6 *Glyndebourne, A History of the Festival Opera* by Spike Hughes (new ed.), David & Charles, 1981

7 *The Daily Telegraph*, 4 May 1937

8 *Truth*, 26 May 1937

9 Rudolf Bing, letter to John Christie, 29 September 1937

10 Audrey Christie, letter to John Christie, 19 July 1937

5. The gardens

1 John Christie, recording for the BBC, 1 July 1957

2 *John Christie of Glyndebourne* by Wilfrid Blunt, London, 1968

3 Audrey Christie, letter to John Christie, 11 November 1932

4 Peter Gellhorn, interview with Carole Rosen for the Glyndebourne Oral History project, 8 May 1991

6. Reawakening

1 Ralph Nicholson played viola with the London Symphony Orchestra at Glyndebourne in 1938 and 1939

2 Sir George Christie, conversation with Rosy Runciman, 4 May 1993

3 Jack Brymer, interview with John Amis for the Glyndebourne Oral History project, 25 February 1992

4 Hope Bagenal, letter to his daughter, Kate, 28 March 1950

5 Leslie Fairweather, conversation with Rosy Runciman, 26 February 1993

6 Jack Brymer, interview with John Amis, *op. cit.*

7 June Dandridge, Stage Manager, Stage Director and Production Manager 1951-82, interview with Noel Goodwin for the Glyndebourne Oral History project, 10 January 1992

8 Moran Caplat, General Manager of Glyndebourne, 1946-81, conversation with Rosy Runciman, 12 March 1993

9 Arthur Southerden, Stage Crew, 1934-39, conversation with Rosy Runciman, 13 May 1993

10 John Christie, foreword to 1952 Glyndebourne programme book

11 John Christie, letter to Major General Daunt, 27 October 1955

7. A new vision

1 Edmund Burke *Reflections on the Revolution in France, 1729-1797*

2 John Christie to Carl Ebert, 1934. Quoted in interview with Carl Ebert for the BBC, 1 June 1955

Acknowledgments

There are a number of people whom I would like to thank for their help with this volume. Many former employees and their relatives provided historical information amongst them John Bagenal, John Edwards, Monica Edwards, Leslie Fairweather, Mrs Jock Gough, Arthur Howell, the late Janet Moores, Mrs Bernard Sharp, Stuart Sisterson, Arthur Southerden, Peter and Margaret Thorpe, Reg Tribe and Jason Warre.

I would also like to thank John Kay of the Ringmer History Group and Christopher Whittick of the East Sussex County Record Office for answering many questions concerning the history of the Glyndebourne Estate.

On the photographic side thanks are due to Philip de Bay and Tom Reeves for their skilled work in copying old photographs and drawings. A great debt of gratitude is owed to Richard Davies, Gus Christie and Joel Hopkins for their dedicated work on site throughout the demolition of the old and building of the new Opera Houses. Without them this book would not have been possible.

Geoff Gash, previously Glyndebourne Site Manager for Bovis Construction, and Alan Lansdell, who took over as Site Manager in January 1993, did much to improve our understanding of the nature of construction work and allowed us frequent access to take photographs.

At Glyndebourne I have received unfailing help and support from George Christie, Helen O'Neill and Joanna Townsend all of whom read and made constructive comments on the text. The former General Administrator, Moran Caplat, has also patiently answered my queries.

Many people at Thames and Hudson have assisted with this project, but in particular Stanley Baron, Thomas Neurath and Ian Mackenzie-Kerr.

On a personal note I would like to thank Humphrey Hawksley who did much to encourage the idea of *Glyndebourne: Building a Vision* at its outset and thereby greatly assisted in turning it into a reality.

Finally my deepest thanks to my co-author, Marcus Binney, for stepping in at short notice to write a piece so attuned to the excitement of building a new opera house.

ROSY RUNCIMAN
March 1994

My thanks are due to all those who gave freely of their time to explain their role in the rebuilding project: they are all cited in the text. Madeleine Cooper kindly supplied me with plentiful background material at short notice. In addition I owe a special debt of gratitude to my co-author Rosy Runciman for help of every kind.

MARCUS BINNEY
March 1994

Picture Credits

There are several people we would like to thank for allowing us to use illustrations of designs or paintings in their possession (the numbers refer to pages in the book):

Peter Andrews 24; Sir George Christie 14–17, 121; Paul Daniel 152; Leslie Esterman 72; Mrs Irene Fife 152; James Sassoon 73

The drawing on p. 96 is reproduced from *Architecture, Actor and Audience* by Iain Mackintosh by kind permission of Routledge & Kegan Paul Ltd.

We would also like to thank the following copyright holders:

Associated Press 51, 66; John Bagenal 36; Robert Bates 121; Bill Brandt 39, 40; Elizabeth Bury 81; Sir Hugh Casson – Contents page, 24, 68; Sir George Christie 22, 23; Gus Christie 6, 21, 22, 23, 28, 86, 87, 102, 106, 115, 116, 118, 119, 122, 123, 125, 126, 127, 132, 136, 139, 140, 142, 143, 147, 148, 151; Beryl Cook 76; Country Life 23, 66; Daily Herald 26, 41, 47; Richard Davies – Frontispiece, 11, 17, 20, 84, 87, 88, 93, 94, 101, 103, 104, 106, 108, 109, 112, 131, 136, 137, 143, 144, 145, 150, 159; J. W. Debenham 57; Lila de Nobili 69; William Dudley 68; East Sussex County Record Office 30; Rolf Gérard 72; Glyndebourne Archive 21, 26, 28, 31, 32, 34, 35, 38, 40, 46, 48, 49, 56, 71; Jacqui Gordon (based on a design by Mary Keen) 115; Guy Gravett 15, 16, 29, 62, 67, 74, 75, 78, 80, 82, 83, 153; Kenneth Green 38, 58; Herb Greer 67; John Gunter 152; Birkin Haward 110; Joel Hopkins 94, 100, 107, 117, 118, 124, 128, 146; Michael Hopkins & Partners 9, 91, 98, 99, 100, 120, 134, 135; Richard Hudson 153; Hulton Deutsch 74; Illustrated London News 54, 55; A. F. Kersting 12, 44, 65; Osbert Lancaster 60, 77; London News Agency 42, 43, 50, 58; E. A. Meyer 59; Caspar Neher 53; Ira Nowinski 82; John Piper 73; RCHME 25, 83; RIBA 19; Reeves of Lewes 33, 35, 48, 79; Reeves/Sussex Archaeological Society 16; Ringmer History Study Group 157; Royal College of Music 27; Rosy Runciman 114, 130; Robin Snell 124; Lord Snowdon 72; Sport and General 59; Theatre Projects Consultants 96, 97; Peter Thomas 64; The Times 43, 58, 70; Michael Wilford & Partners 8, 92; Hamish Wilson 37, 52; Roger Wood 75

Chronologies

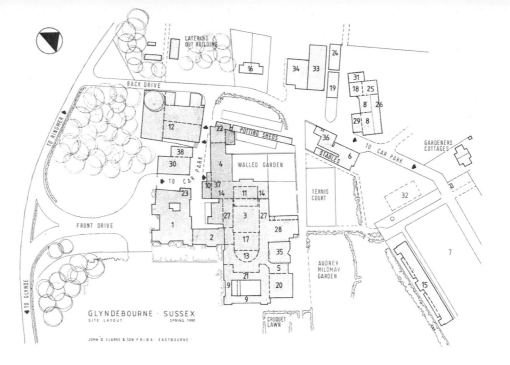

	The Private House	1
1919/20	The Organ Room	2
1933/34	The Opera House:	
	Auditorium (300 stalls seats)	
	with private box at back	
	Dressing rooms for principals	
	on either side of stalls	3
	Dining Hall and Kitchen	4
1935	Scenery dock	5
	Scenery store	6
	Car park	7
	Garage/Scenery store	8
	Dressing room block with	
	Green Room and temporary	
	connecting passages to opera	
	house	9
1936	Garden outbuildings converted	
	into offices	10
1937	Auditorium widened by	
	incorporating space of former	
	dressing rooms at side and adding	
	Red and Blue foyers	3,27
	Balcony added and private box	
	moved to centre of balcony	11
	Total 433 seats excluding	
	private box	
	Wallop dining halls and kitchen	12
	Cyclorama wall built and space	
	behind roofed over for scenery	
	dock	13
	Former terrace roofed over to	
	provide Covered Way	14
	Accommodation for seasonal staff	15

	Houses for Chief Technician and	
	Gardener	16
1938	Enlargement of balcony	11
	Additional boxes and seats	
	added at stalls level	3
	Total 527 seats excluding private	
	box	
	Flytower built over stage	17
1939	Ten seats added in stalls	3
	Total 537 seats excluding private	
	box	
1951	Private box moved to back of stalls	3
	Increase of seats in balcony	11
	Total 592 seats	
1953	Auditorium roof rebuilt and	
	supporting columns moved outwards	
	Balcony extended at back	
	Accommodation in boxes behind	
	stalls increased	
	Total 718 seats	
	Proscenium opening enlarged	3,11
1955	Open garage	18
	Garage/Scenery store converted	
	to chorus rehearsal room	8
1957	Ceiling of auditorium rebuilt	
	Private box moved to back of	
	stalls and seats added at back	
	of balcony	3,11
	Total 762 seats	
	Scenery store	19
1959	Rehearsal stage with wardrobe	
	and general storage beneath	20
1960	Wardrobe workroom extended	21

Property workshop moved from backstage	22
Staff accommodation added to house	23
1961 Scenery store	24
1962 Rehearsal room	25
Wardrobe store	26
1963 Five new boxes added at balcony level. Offices built behind boxes above Red and Blue foyers Total 798 seats	27
1964 Sixth box added at balcony level Total 804 seats	27
Proscenium opening enlarged	3
1968 Height of cyclorama increased	13
1973 Conversion of existing wing into Lily Davis Rehearsal Room and Staff Bar	28
1974 Conversion and extension into scenery workshop and rehearsal room	8,29
1974–80 Conversion to rehearsal rooms and offices of harness room and domestic outbuildings	30
1975 Property store	31
Extension of basement understage to form new bandroom	17
1976 Balcony re-seated at steeper rake	11
Establishment of WD and HO Wills Marquee Pavilion in car park	32
1977 Auditorium redecorated and reseated Total 845 seats	3,11

1978	Flytower re-shingled	17
1979	Scenery store, first phase	33
1980	Conversion and extension into Tuff Turton rehearsal room complex	18,25,8
	Extensions and improvements to seasonal staff accommodation	15
1981	Scenery store, second phase	33
1982–3	Backstage extension, new scene dock	35
1983	Lighting projection room above balcony extended	11
1984	Tailoring and wigs workrooms built on site of former scenery store	6,36
1986	New offices above Box Office	37
1987	Organ Room roof re-tiled	2
	Stage and backstage areas re-floored	13,17
1988	Archive store built above garage	38
1991	Scenery workshop converted into property workshop	29
	Mildmay Hall, Property Workshop, Potting Sheds, Walled Garden demolished	4,22
	Tailoring and wigs workrooms demolished	6,36
1992	Plashett huts converted into offices for duration of theatre rebuild	15
	Theatre and surrounding buildings demolished to make way for new opera house	3,11,17,13 14,37,10, 275,35,28

New Opera House Construction Programme

July 1988
Architects approached to submit design ideas

October 1988
MHP shortlisted to submit design proposals

February 1989
MHP appointed to design the new Opera House

December 1990
Scheme Design Approval

7 May 1991
Glyndebourne announces 'go ahead'

27 July 1991
Start on Site Phase 1A
(backstage and rehearsal stage)

August 1992
Demolition of old opera house

5 August 1992
Start on Site Phase 1B
(stage, flytower, auditorium and front of house)

31 December 1993
Project Completion

28 May 1994
New Opera House First Night

A group photograph of the employees at John Christie's company, Ringmer Building Works, taken in the 1920s

Project Team

Eric Gabriel, Alan Lansdell, Norman Byrne, Robin Snell, Ray Hague and Stas Brzeski reviewing the practical completion documentation on the day before the Opera House was officially handed over to Glyndebourne, 30 December 1993

Client Project Manager	Eric Gabriel
Architect	**Michael Hopkins & Partners** Michael Hopkins Patty Hopkins Robin Snell (Project architect)
Structural & Services Engineers	**Ove Arup & Partners** John Thornton John Berry John Turzynski Stas Brzeski
Acoustic Consultants	**Arup Acoustics** Derek Sugden Rob Harris Raf Orlowski Helen Thornton
Theatre Consultant	**Theatre Projects Consultants** Iain Mackintosh Alan Russell Anne Minors
Cost Consultant	**Gardiner & Theobald** Michael Coates Peter Coxall Gary Faulkner
Construction Manager	**Bovis Construction Limited** Christopher Spackman Les Chatfield Alan Lansdell
Theatre Advisor	John Bury
Construction Advisors	**Stanhope Properties Plc** Stuart Lipton Paul Lewis
Landscape Advisor	Lady Mary Keen

Trade Contractors

Substructure Phase 1A	Geoffrey Osborne Civil Engineering Ltd
Substructure & Superstructure Phase 1B	O'Rourke Civil & Structural Engineering Ltd
Mechanical, Electrical and Plumbing Services	Matthew Hall Limited
Brickwork and Blockwork	Irvine Whitlock Limited
Structural Steelwork phase 1B	Hollandia bv
Lead Roofing	Broderick Structures Limited
Auditorium Fitout	Cheesman Interiors Limited
Stage Equipment, Orchestra & Cloth Lifts, Special Acoustic Doors	Tele-Stage Associates (UK) Ltd
Precast Concrete Supply 1A	Dynaspan (UK) Limited
Precast Concrete Supply 1B	Trent Concrete Structures Ltd
Brick Supply	Selborne Brick Limited
Structural Steelwork 1A and Auditorium Raised Floor Steelwork	Littlehampton Welding Ltd
General Metalwork	Cromwell of Reading

Auditorium Seating	Audience Systems Ltd
Toilet Fit-out	Grant Westfield Ltd
Back of House Fit-Out	Wilson Fitting Out Limited
Sound & Communications	Shuttlesound
Stage Lighting	Strand Lighting
Electricity Mains and Substation	Seeboard Plc
Gas Mains	British Gas Plc
Demolition and Groundwork	Best Demolition
Sewage Treatment Plant	Country Drainage
Security Installation	General Security Limited
Raised Floors	Metier Flooring Limited
Lead Cladding Panels & Cills	Weather Tight Systems Ltd
Goods & Passenger Lift	Otis Elevators Limited
Vehicle Lift	Glantree Engineering Limited
Roof Glazing	ESB Services Limited
Fly Tower Lead Cladding	Kershaw Mechanical Services Ltd
Gutter Lining	Rutherford & Morgan
Metal Doors	Bostwick Doors (UK) Limited
Foyer Fabric Roof	Landrell Fabric Engineering Ltd
Glazed Screens	T & W Ide Limited
Floor Finishes	Derry Treanor
Auditorium Raised Floor (Foyer)	Surrey Steel Buildings Limited
Signage	The HB Sign Company Limited
Foyer & Shop Fitout	Sherlock Interiors Contracting
Dry Lining	Jonathan James Limited
Tableau Curtains	Mick Tomlin Limited
Service Lift	Associated Lift Services Limited
Electrical Services Diversions	East Sussex Electric
Mechanical Services Diversions	Ashdown Mechanical Services
Air Handling Units	Redbro Limited
Chiller Plant	Trane (UK) Limited
Installation of Windows	South East Fixing
Louvred Window Supply	Beta Naco
Window Supply	Allday Windows Limited
Ironmongery Supply	Allgood Hardware Limited
Firestopping	West Anglia Insulation Ltd
Loading Bay Doors	Clark Door Limited
Auditorium Raised Floor-Metalwork Design	Holt & Wootten
Auditorium Raised Floor-Metalwork Fabrication	Playfield Engineering Ltd
Landscaping	Landscape Management Construction
Site Catering	Russell Smith
Reclaimed Pitch Pine Supply	Jeremy Nelson
Final Clean	Cleaningwise Limited
Architects for the new Scenery Store/Wardrobe Block	The Miller Bourne Partnership
Building contractors for the Scenery Store/Wardrobe Block	James Longley & Co Ltd
Architects for the conversion of the old Dressing Room Block into rehearsal studios/company cafeteria extension, etc.	The Miller Bourne Partnership
Building contractors for the conversion of the old Dressing Room Block into rehearsal studios/company cafeteria extension, etc.	James Longley & Co Ltd

Index *Page numbers in **bold** type refer to illustrations*